Pittsburgh Series in Bibliography

Ross Macdonald/ Kenneth Millar

A DESCRIPTIVE BIBLIOGRAPHY

Matthew J. Bruccoli

UNIVERSITY OF
PITTSBURGH PRESS
1983

Published by the University of Pittsburgh Press, Pittsburgh, Pa. 15260
Copyright © 1983, University of Pittsburgh Press
All rights reserved
Feffer and Simons, Inc., London
Manufactured in the United States of America

Library of Congress Cataloging in Publication Data

Bruccoli, Matthew Joseph, 1931–
  Ross Macdonald/Kenneth Millar, a descriptive bibliography.

  (Pittsburgh series in bibliography)
  Includes index.
  1. Macdonald, Ross, 1915–   —Bibliography.
  I. Title. II. Series.
  Z8532.386.B78   1983   [PS3525.I486]   016.813′52   83-1398
  ISBN 0-8229-3482-5

For Nancy and Frederick Hetzel: 12–14–57

Contents

Acknowledgments

GOOD bibliographies are collaborations. I am indebted to the following: Capra Press, Aubrey Davis and Patricia Cork (Hughes Massie), Ashbel Green (Alfred A. Knopf), Muriel Hamilton (Hampton Books), Arthur Kaye, Lord John Press, David Monaghan, Mystery Writers of America, Dorothy Olding (Harold Ober Associates), Otto Penzler (Mysterious Book Shop), Anthony Rota (Bertram Rota), Ralph Bruno Sipper (Joseph the Provider), Michael Van Blaricum (The Bookstalker), and Elizabeth Walter (William Collins Sons).

The Interlibrary Loan Department staff at the Thomas Cooper Library, University of South Carolina, proved—as always—a marvel of forbearance and cooperation: Harriet Oglesbee, Lori Finger, Susan Bradley, and Beth Woodard. The British Library, the Library of Congress, and the U.S. Copyright Office are good places to work.

The typescript was vetted by William Cagle (Lilly Library, Indiana University), Joel Myerson (University of South Carolina), Charles Mann (Pattee Library, Pennsylvania State University), and Roger Berry (University of California–Irvine).

Meredith Walker and Catherine Coleman typed and retyped; Mrs. Coleman prepared the index. Heather Barker and Michael Mullen checked and fetched. I am fortunate to be at the University of South Carolina, and I am particularly obligated to Professor George Geckle, Chairman of the Department of English.

Frederick A. Hetzel, Director of the University of Pittsburgh Press, makes this series possible.

Introduction

PUBLICATION is the essential act of scholarship, but all bibliographies are works in progress.

Kenneth Millar's books have been published as by Kenneth Millar, John Macdonald, John Ross Macdonald, and Ross Macdonald. Whenever a later edition or printing of a title appeared with the name of the author changed from that of the first publication, the information is noted.

FORMAT

Section A lists chronologically all books and pamphlets by Kenneth Millar/ Ross Macdonald, including all printings of all editions in English. The numbering system for section A designates the edition and the printing for each entry. Thus for *The Underground Man,* A 23.2.a indicates that the volume described is the twenty-third book by Millar/Macdonald (A 23) and is the first printing of the second edition (2.a).

Section AA lists chronologically the omnibus volumes of novels by Millar/ Macdonald.

Section B lists chronologically all books and pamphlets in which material by Millar/Macdonald appeared for the first time. Previously unpublished items are so noted. The first printings only of these items are described.

Section C lists chronologically the first appearances of all Millar/Macdonald contributions to periodicals and newspapers—including interviews and public statements.

Section D lists alphabetically blurbs by Millar/Macdonald printed in ads and on dust jackets or wrappers.

Appendix 1: Compiler's Notes.

Appendix 2: Books about Millar/Macdonald.

TERMS AND METHODS

Edition. All the copies of a book printed from a single setting of type— including all reprintings from standing type, from plates, or by photo-offset.

Printing. All the copies of a book printed at one time (without removing the type or plates from the press).

States. States occur only within single printings and are created by an alteration not affecting the conditions of publication to *some* copies of a given printing (by stop-press correction or cancellation of leaves). There are no states in Millar's/Macdonald's books.[1]

---

1. There cannot be a first state without a second state; there cannot be a first issue without a second issue.

Issue. Issues occur only within single printings and are created by an alteration affecting the conditions of publication or sale to *some* copies of given printing (usually a title-page alteration or by a change in the certificate of limitation). Issues are designated by asterisks: A 25.1.a* identifies the trade issue of the first printing of *On Crime Writing.*

Edition, printing, state, and *issue* are normally restricted to the sheets of the books. In strict usage, binding and dust-jacket variants have no bearing on these terms, but exceptions occur in this bibliography. Some of the sheets of the third Bantam Books printing of *The Dark Tunnel* were sold in England with Corgi Books wrappers, thereby creating an issue (A 1.4.c*). When *A Collection of Reviews* was published simultaneously in 300 numbered/signed copies and 50 specially bound numbered/signed copies, the publisher's intention was to market two separate issues (A 30.1.a and A 30.1.a*). In these cases the term *binding issue* has been applied.

Dust jackets for section A have been described in less detail here than in other bibliographies in this series; but every located jacket has been illustrated, and the principal colors have been noted. Unless *wrappers* is specified, a book is clothbound. The spines of bindings and dust jackets are printed horizontally unless otherwise noted.

For binding-cloth descriptions I have used the method proposed by G. Thomas Tanselle;[2] most of these cloth grains are illustrated in *The Bibliography of American Literature,* ed. Jacob Blanck (New Haven, Conn.: Yale University Press, 1955–).

Color specifications are taken from the *ISCC-NBS Color-Name Charts Illustrated with Centroid Colors* (National Bureau of Standards). In the descriptions of title pages, bindings, and dust jackets, the color of the lettering is always black unless otherwise specified. A color holds for subsequent lines until a color change is stipulated. The style of type is roman, unless otherwise specified.

The term *perfect binding* refers to books in which the pages are held together with adhesive along the spine after the folds have been trimmed, as for most paperbacks.

The locations rubric does not list every copy examined.

Dates provided within brackets do not appear on the title pages. Usually—but not invariably—they are taken from the copyright pages.

Locations are provided by the following symbols:

BL: British Library, London
UC-I: University of California, Irvine
LC: Library of Congress
Lilly: Lilly Library, Indiana University
MJB: Collection of Matthew J. Bruccoli
PSt: Pennsylvania State University
ScU: University of South Carolina

---

2. "The Specifications of Binding Cloth," *The Library* 21 (September 1966), 246–247.

For paperbacks the serial number provided is that of the first printing. Paperback publishers normally change the serial number for later printings, but this information has not been noted.

It is desirable to avoid end-of-line hyphens in bibliographical transcriptions. Because of a measured line, it is impossible to satisfy this requirement in every case. End-of-line hyphens have been avoided wherever possible, and always where a hyphen would create ambiguity.

The University of South Carolina
21 August 1982

A. Separate Publications

A 1 THE DARK TUNNEL

A 1.1.a
First edition, first printing (1944)

KENNETH MILLAR

THE

Dark Tunnel

This is a Red Badge Mystery

DODD, MEAD & COMPANY

New York - 1944

A 1.1.a: 5″ × 7¼″

```
COPYRIGHT, 1944,
By KENNETH MILLAR


ALL RIGHTS RESERVED
NO PART OF THIS BOOK MAY BE REPRODUCED IN ANY FORM
WITHOUT PERMISSION IN WRITING FROM THE PUBLISHER

PRINTED IN THE UNITED STATES OF AMERICA
BY THE VAIL-BALLOU PRESS, INC., BINGHAMTON, N. Y.
```

[i–viii] 1–241 [242–244]

[1–14]⁸ [15]⁶ [16]⁸

Contents: p. i: half title; p. ii: announcement of Red Badge contest; p. iii: title; p. iv: copyright; p. v: 'TO THE MEMORY OF | JOHN LEE'; p. vi: blank; p. vii: disclaimer; p. viii: blank; pp. 1–241: text; pp. 242–244: blank.

Typography and paper: 5 7/8″ (6 1/8″) × 3 13/16″. 35 lines per page. Running heads: rectos and versos, 'THE DARK TUNNEL'. Wove paper.

Binding: Deep reddish orange (#36) V-cloth (smooth). Front: '[against black badge] RED BADGE | [detective within circle] | DETECTIVE | DODD | MEAD'. Spine black-stamped: '[horizontal in script] Kenneth | Millar | [vertical in roman] THE DARK TUNNEL | [horizontal in roman] DODD, MEAD | & COMPANY'. White endpapers. Top and bottom edges trimmed.

Dust jacket: Front and spine blue; back white. Front lettered in white and blue shadowed in white, with illustration in blue and white.

Publication: Published 12 September 1944. $2. Copyright #A 182835

Printing: Manufactured by Vail-Ballou Press, Binghamton, N.Y.

Locations: LC (SEP 13 1944); Lilly (dj); MJB (dj).

Note: Abridged in the *Toronto Star Weekly* (1944). Unlocated.

A 1.1.b
First edition, second printing: New York: Dodd, Mead, 1944.

On copyright page: 'Published September 1944 | Second printing September 1944'.

A 1.2.a
Second edition, first printing: New York: Lion, [1950].

#48. Wrappers.

A 1.2.b
Second edition, second printing: Boston: Gregg Press, 1980.

Introduction by Bill Pronzini. Ross Macdonald.

A 1.3
Third edition: I Die Slowly. New York: Lion, [1955].

#LL52. Wrappers.

Dust jacket for A1.1.a

A 1.4.a

Fourth edition, first printing: New York, Toronto, London: Bantam, [1972].

On copyright page: 'Bantam edition published October 1972'.

#N7367. Wrappers. Four printings. Ross Macdonald.

A 1.4.c*

Fourth edition, third printing, English binding issue: Bantam sheets in Corgi Books wrappers, 1973?

ISBN #0-552-67367-6. Ross Macdonald.

A 2 TROUBLE FOLLOWS ME

A 2.1
First edition, only printing (1946)

TROUBLE FOLLOWS ME

BY

KENNETH MILLAR

Author of
The Dark Tunnel

This is a Red Badge Mystery

NEW YORK

DODD, MEAD & COMPANY

1946

A 2.1: 5^{1}/$_{8}$″ × 7^{3}/$_{8}$″

COPYRIGHT, 1946,
BY KENNETH MILLAR

ALL RIGHTS RESERVED
NO PART OF THIS BOOK MAY BE REPRODUCED IN ANY FORM
WITHOUT PERMISSION IN WRITING FROM THE PUBLISHER

PRINTED IN THE UNITED STATES OF AMERICA
BY THE VAIL-BALLOU PRESS, INC., BINGHAMTON, N. Y.

[i–viii] [1–2] 3–44 [45–46] 47–75 [76–78] 79–145 [146–148] 149–206 [207–208]
$[1–6]^{16}$ $[7]^{12}$

Contents: p. i: half title; p. ii: announcement for Red Badge contest; p. iii: title; p. iv: copyright; p. v.: 'TO | DONALD PEARCE'; p. vi: blank; p. vii: contents; p. viii: blank; p. 1: part title; p. 2: disclaimer; pp. 3–44: text; p. 45: part title; p. 46: blank; pp. 47–75: text; p. 76: blank; p. 77: part title; p. 78: blank; pp. 79–145: text; p. 146: blank; p. 147: part title; p. 148: blank; pp. 149–206: text; pp. 207–208: blank.

Typography and paper: $5^{3}/_{4}''$ $(5^{15}/_{16}'')$ × $3^{13}/_{16}''$. 35 lines per page. No running heads. Wove paper.

Binding: Very light gray olive (#109) paper-covered boards with V-pattern (smooth). Front: '[against black badge] RED BADGE | [detective within circle] | DETECTIVE | DODD | MEAD'. Spine blackstamped: [horizontal] KENNETH | MILLAR | [vertical] TROUBLE FOLLOWS ME | [horizontal] DODD, MEAD | & COMPANY'. White endpapers. Top and bottom edges trimmed.

Dust jacket: Front and spine illustrated in gray and yellow; back white. Front lettered in yellow and white. Signed: McMillen.

Publication: Published 20 August 1946. $2. Copyright #A 5525.

Printing: Manufactured by Vail-Ballou Press, Binghamton, N.Y.

Locations: LC (AUG 9 1946); Lilly (dj); MJB (dj); UC-I.

A 2.2
Second edition: New York: Lion, [1950].

#47. Wrappers.

A 2.3
Third edition: Night Train. New York: Lion, [1955].

#LL40. Wrappers.

A 2.4.a
Fourth edition: New York, Toronto, London: Bantam, [1972].

#N7189. *On copyright page: 'Bantam edition published September 1972'.*

Wrappers. 3 printings. Ross Macdonald.

Dust jacket for A.2.1

A 2.4.c*
Fourth edition, third printing, English binding issue: Bantam sheets in Corgi Books wrappers, 1973?

ISBN #0-552-67189-4. Ross Macdonald.

A 3 BLUE CITY

A 3.1
First edition, only printing (1947)

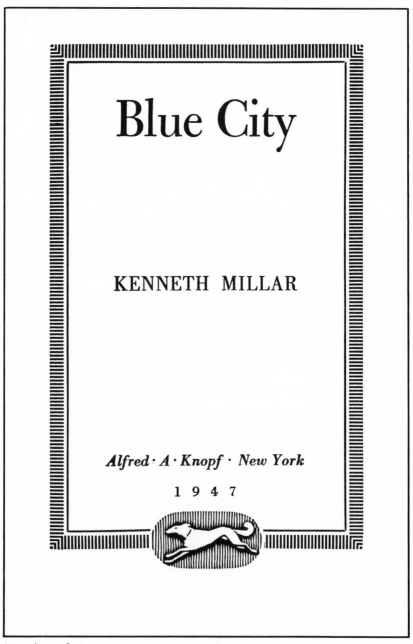

A 3.1: 5^{1}/4″ × 7^{7}/$_{16}$″

[i–viii] [1–2] 3–276 [277–280]

[1–9]^{16}

Contents: pp. i–ii: blank; p. iii: half title; p. iv: blank; p. v: title; p. vi: copyright; p. vii: 'To | ROBERT FORD'; p. viii: blank; p. 1: half title; p. 2: blank; pp. 3–276: text; p. 277: blank; p. 278: note on type; pp. 279–280: blank.

Typography and paper: 5½" (5^{15}/₁₆") × 3⁹/₁₆". 30 or 31 lines per page. Running heads: rectos and versos, '*Blue City*'. Wove paper.

Binding: Deep reddish orange (#36) V-cloth (smooth) stamped in blue. Front: '[within decorated frame] KM'. Spine: '[decoration] | *Blue* | *City* | [decoration] | *Kenneth* | *Millar* | KNOPF'. Back: borzoi within decorated frame. White endpapers. Top and bottom edges trimmed. Top edge stained gray.

Dust jacket: Front and spine red and blue; back white. Front lettered in red and white with black and white art.

Publication: Published 18 August 1947. $2.50. Copyright #A 14596.

Printing: Composition, printing, and binding by H. Wolff, New York.

Locations: LC (JUN 20 1947); Lilly (dj); MJB (dj); UC-I (dj).

Dust jacket for A 3.1

A 3.2
First English edition, only printing (1949)

BLUE CITY

by
KENNETH MILLAR

CASSELL AND COMPANY LTD.
LONDON, TORONTO, MELBOURNE, SYDNEY
& WELLINGTON

A 3.2: 4⁷/₈″ × 7¹/₄″

```
THIS BOOK IS PRODUCED IN
COMPLETE CONFORMITY WITH THE
AUTHORIZED ECONOMY STANDARDS

First published in Great Britain 1949

PRINTED  IN  GREAT  BRITAIN  BY
NORTHUMBERLAND PRESS LIMITED
GATESHEAD ON TYNE
F.1248
```

[1–6] 7–230 [231–232]
[A]^{16} B–G^{16} H^4

Contents: p. 1: half title; p. 2: blank; p. 3: title; p. 4: copyright; p. 5: dedication; p. 6: blank; pp. 7–231: text; p. 232: blank.

Typography and paper: 5^5/$_8$″ (5^3/$_4$″) × 3^1/$_2$″. 37 lines per page. No running heads. Wove paper.

Binding: Gray purplish blue (#204) V-cloth (smooth). Spine stamped in very pale purplish blue: '[script] Blue | City | [roman] KENNETH | MILLAR | CASSELL'. Off-white endpapers. All edges trimmed.

Dust jacket: Pink and white script against dark blue background on front and spine; lettering in yellow and white.

Publication: 3,962 copies of the first printing. Published 11 October 1949. 8/6.

Printing: See copyright page.

Locations: BL (11 OCT 49); MJB (dj).

A 3.3
Third edition: New York: Dell, [1949].

#363. Wrappers. Reprinted 1950.

A 3.4.a
Fourth edition: New York: Bantam, [1958].

#1839. Wrappers. Two printings in 1958 and third printing in 1968. Ross Macdonald.

A 3.4.b
Fourth edition, Canadian printings: Reprinted by Bantam in Canada, 1958 and 1974.

Not seen.

A 3.5
Fifth edition: London: Transworld Corgi, [1962].

Wrappers. 33,020 copies. Ross Macdonald.

8/6 net

Blue City

KENNETH MILLAR

Blue City
KENNETH MILLAR
CASSELL

BLUE CITY

In 1946, after many years' absence, John Weather returns to Blue City to find that his father—the one-time Mayor—had been murdered on the street two years before. For political reasons among the conflicting forces which now rule the place, the murder has been hushed up and the murderer never found. The City, as Weather finds it on his return, is one of evil and corruption, and corruption, as he also discovers, is something which time injected into a political organism is bound to spread. And this is what has happened in Blue City which is rotting from the top. It is an ugly City now; too ugly even for the turn and worthen who have made it that way and its corruption reveals John Weather into action on its own terms.

Kenneth Millar writes with uncompromising toughness and spares us no reality. His world is one of brutal virtue; his people without pity or remorse. But this is not toughness for the sake of toughness. It is a harsh and vivid picture of a brutal side of life, focused before us with pitiless charity like a sudden light in a shameful room. And in the nakedness of its tearing reality and in a manner which is not easily forgotten, we are faced with the brutal implications of these people's lives, and a disquieting disturbance for some sort of truth which they contain.

Kenneth Millar

Dust jacket for A3.2

A 3.6

Sixth edition: London: Collins, [1981].

Crime Club Famous Firsts Collection. Ross Macdonald.

Note: Condensed in *Esquire* 34 (Aug.–Sept. 1950), 86–96, 94–117.

A 4 THE THREE ROADS

A 4.1
First edition, only printing (1948)

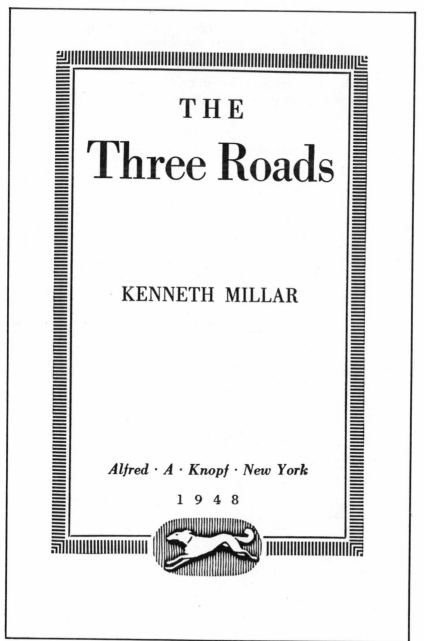

A 4.1: 5¹/₈″ × 7¹/₂″

[i–xii] [1–2] 3–44 [45–46] 47–77 [78–80] 81–111 [112–114] 115–223 [224–228]

$[1-6]^{16}$ $[7]^{8}$ $[8]^{16}$

Contents: p. i: blank; p. ii: card page; p. iii: half title; p. iv: blank; p. v: title; p. vi: copyright; p. vii: 'To | MARGARET'; p. viii: blank; p. ix: 4-line epigraph from *Oedipus Tyrannus;* p. x: blank; p. xi: contents; p. xii: blank; p. 1: part title; p. 2: blank; pp. 3–44: text; p. 45: part title; p. 46; blank; pp. 47–77: text; p. 78: blank; p. 79: part title; p. 80: blank; pp. 81–111: text; p. 112: blank; p. 113: part title; p. 114: blank; pp. 115–223: text; p. 224: blank; p. 225: note on type; pp. 226–228: blank.

Typography and paper: 5⁹/₁₆″ (5¹⁵/₁₆″) × 3⁵/₈″. 35 lines per page. Running heads: rectos, part title; versos, 'The Three Roads'. Wove paper.

Binding: Medium yellow brown (#77) paper-covered boards with B-pattern (linen); stamped in blue. Front: '[within decorated frame] KM'. Spine: '[decoration] | The | Three | Roads | [decoration] | Kenneth | Millar | KNOPF'. Back: borzoi within decorated frame. White endpapers. Top and bottom edges trimmed. Top edge stained blue. Also noted with top edge unstained.

Dust jacket: Front red, blue, and white; spine black; back white. Front lettered in black with black and white art.

Publication: Published 7 June 1948. $2.50. Copyright A 23067.

Printing: Composed, printed, and bound by H. Wolff, New York.

Locations: LC (MAY 26 1948); Lilly (dj); MJB (dj); PSt (t.e. unstained); UC-I (dj).

A 4.2
Second edition: New York: Dell, [1949].

#497. Wrappers.

Dust jacket for A.4.1

$2.50 net

THE THREE ROADS
by KENNETH MILLAR

This is the tale of a man whose sanity and chance for happiness depend on his ability to recapture his unremembered past. "Forget the past," cries Paula, who loves him but doesn't understand. "I've got to remember it first," is Bret's grim answer. Any reader who stares back into the past with Bret will remain trapped at his side, for living at the core of the darkness of this man's memory is a brutal, unsolved murder.

Kenneth Millar, who has aptly been likened to James M. Cain and his brothers for the fast-moving, hardchiseled quality of his writing, starts his latest work at a slow, steady pitch that builds up and up till tension and suspense reach an unbearable high, and then—with all the sudden surefire speed and violence of a roller-coaster descent—takes his story into action.

JACKET DESIGN BY ARTHUR HAWKINS, JR.

THE THREE ROADS

KENNETH MILLAR

A NOVEL OF SUSPENSE BY
KENNETH MILLAR
AUTHOR OF BLUE CITY

BORZOI BOOKS

ALFRED A KNOPF

(spine) THE THREE ROADS — KENNETH MILLAR

SOME BORZOI FICTION

★ DUPEE BLUES by Dale Curran

A blues ballad brought to life—the story of a nice guy, a simple guy, a trombone player who played his music from the heart, and of Betty, the singer in the band, who sang her music sweet but from the hips. In the pit of your stomach as you start reading, a small cold ball grows and grows because you know what has to happen.

★ STOKERS' MESS by Arne Skouen

The story of two frenzied days in the life of an adolescent messboy in the stokers' hold of a freighter off the east coast of Africa—a daydreaming boy of fifteen whose coming of age is condensed into a few climactic hours during an all-night brawl.

★ ASYLUM FOR THE QUEEN by Mildred Jordan

The time is that of the French Revolution, the story that of a group of aristocrats who plot to rescue the royal family from imprisonment in Paris and bring them to a Pennsylvania colony named Asylum until they can return to France in triumph. A moving and thrilling story.

★ MAN IS STRONG by Corrado Alvaro

One of the leading Italian novelists of our day here gives us a compelling and graphic story dealing with the effect of police regimentation and fear upon modern man.

★ BULLIVANT AND THE LAMBS by I. Compton-Burnett

I. Compton-Burnett's latest novel is a ferocious comedy of manners couched mostly in dialogue of astonishing brilliance and subtlety. An uproarious and sinister tale of Bullivant the omnipotent butler and the incredible brood of Horace Lamb.

ALFRED · A · KNOPF · PUBLISHER · NEW · YORK

Olga Coman

KENNETH MILLAR was born at Los Gatos, California, on December 13, 1915, of mixed Scotch-Canadian and Pennsylvania Dutch ancestry. After growing up in western Canada he attended the University of Western Ontario, from which he was graduated in 1938. The day after his graduation he married a Canadian girl, who has written mystery stories and novels under the name of Margaret Millar. After a period during which he taught in high school and later held a fellowship at the University of Michigan, in 1944 he entered the Navy and became a communications officer on an escort carrier. Since his release from the Navy in the spring of 1946 Millar has been living in California with his wife and young daughter. He is the author of three novels, The Dark Tunnel, Trouble Follows Me, and Blue City.

A 4.3
First English edition, only printing (1950)

THE THREE ROADS

by

KENNETH MILLAR

CASSELL AND COMPANY LTD.
LONDON, TORONTO, MELBOURNE, SYDNEY
& WELLINGTON

A 4.3: 4^1/$_4$″ × 7^3/$_{16}$″

```
First published in Great Britain 1950

SET IN 10-PT BASKERVILLE TYPE AND
PRINTED IN GREAT BRITAIN BY
NORTHUMBERLAND PRESS LIMITED
GATESHEAD ON TYNE
F.250
```

[1—10] 11–230 [231–232]

[A]^{16} B–G^{16} H^4

Contents: p. 1: half title; p. 2: card page; p. 3: title; p. 4: copyright; p. 5: dedication; p. 6: epigraph; p. 7: contents; p. 8: blank; p. 9: section title; p. 10: blank; pp. 11–231: text; p. 232: blank.

Typography and paper: 5^{11}/$_{16}$″ (5^7/$_8$″) × 3^5/$_8$″. 37 lines per page. No running heads. Wove paper.

Binding: Black V-cloth (smooth). Spine silverstamped: '*THE | THREE | ROADS | Kenneth | Millar | Cassell*'. White endpapers. All edges trimmed.

Dust jacket: Front and spine lettered in white; front illustration in shades of gray.

Publication: 3,216 copies of the first printing. Published September 1950. 9/6.

Printing: See copyright page.

Locations: BL (11 SEP 50); UC-I (dj).

A4.4.a
Fourth edition, first printing: New York: Bantam, [1960].

#A2096. Wrappers. Reprinted 1968. Ross Macdonald.

A4.4.b
Fourth edition, Canadian printing: †New York, Toronto, London: Bantam books, [1968].

#F3665. *On copyright page: '2nd printing . . . March 1968*'. Wrappers. Ross Macdonald.

A4.5
Fifth edition: London: Transworld Corgi, [1962].

Wrappers. 28,735 copies. Ross Macdonald.

A4.6.a
Sixth edition: New York, Toronto, London: Bantam Books, [1974].

#Q8420. Wrappers. Four printings, 1974–1983. Ross Macdonald.

---

†Entries identified as Canadian printings bear the copyright page slug 'PRINTED IN CANADA'.

This is the story of a man whose sanity and chance for happiness depend on his ability to recapture his unremembered past. The Doctors know that the reason for Brett Taylor's mental suffering is guilt, but they point out that although guilt is normally thought of as the result of sin, it may really be its cause; their theory being that the sense of some guilt may have worked on Brett until he was driven to crime.

Following the belief that nothing in a person's life is ever really forgotten — in a sense that with the right encouragement any memory can be recalled—Brett is determined to trace his life back to the point where his memory failed, and to find the reason for it. Paula, who knows what happened, believes that his mental health is not strong enough to stand the strain of knowing what was done. She knows, and is being blackmailed because she knows, that the cause of all his suffering is the mental shirking of a brutal unsolved murder, and she is very much afraid.

9|6 NET

THE THREE ROADS

KENNETH MILLAR

Author of BLUE CITY

CASSELL

CASSELL MYSTERIES

REGINALD CAMPBELL
Death by Apparition
Brainstorm

ROY HUGGINS
The Double Take
Too Late for Tears

STUART TOWNE
Death out of Thin Air

HUGH CLEVELY
Not Nice People
No Peace for Archer
More Trouble for Archer

TOD CLAYMORE
Nest of Vipers
What Else Could I Do?

ALASTAIR SCOBIE
Kangaroo Shoots Man
Murder à la Mozambique

LESTER DENT
Dead at the Take-off
Lady to Kill
Lady Afraid

LUCY CORES
Corpse de Ballet
Painted for the Kill

G. K. CHESTERTON
The Father Brown Omnibus
The Dashiell Hammett Omnibus

MARY ROBERTS RINEHART
The Yellow Room
Haunted Lady
The Wall

ERLE STANLEY GARDNER
The Case of the Gold-Diggers Purse
The Case of the Black-Eyed Blonde
The Case of the Crooked Candle
The Case of the Drowsy Mosquito
The D.A. Calls a Turn
The D.A. Breaks a Seal

RICHARD ELLINGTON
Shoot the Works

KENNETH MILLAR
Blue City

LAWRENCE LARIAR
The Girl with the Frightened Eyes

MARION HOLBROOK
Wanted a Murderess

WILSON TUCKER
The Dove
To Keep or Kill
The Chinese Doll

CAREY MAGOON
I Smell the Devil

Dust jacket for A4.3

A 5 THE MOVING TARGET

A 5.1.a
First edition, first printing (1949)

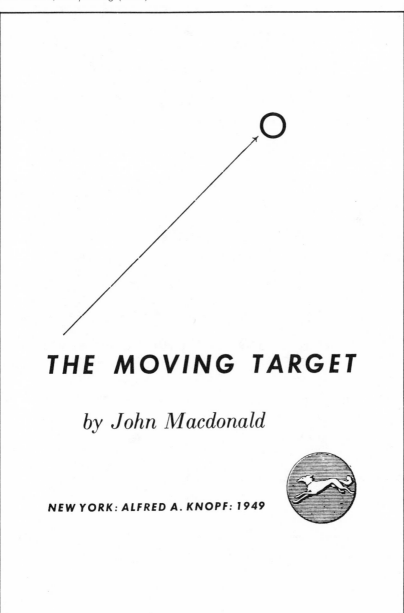

A 5.1.a: 5¹/₈″ × 7¹/₂″

[i–vi] [1–3] 4–245 [246–250]

[1–8]^{16}

Contents: pp. i–ii: blank; p. iii: blurb for *The Moving Target;* p. iv: blank; p. v: title; p. vi: copyright; p. 1: half title; p. 2: blank; pp. 3–245: text; p. 246: blank; p. 247: note on type; pp. 248–250: blank.

Typography and paper: 5⅝″ (5⅞″) × 3⅝″. 31 lines per page. Running heads: rectos and versos, '*THE MOVING TARGET*'. Wove paper.

Binding: Gray reddish orange (#39) cloth with V-pattern (smooth). Front, back and spine stamped in dark green. Front: '[between converging lines leading to bull's eye] 'THE MOVING TARGET'. Spine: '[slanted up] THE | MOVING | TARGET | [bull's eye] | [slanted down] John | [slanted up] Macdonald | [rule] | KNOPF'. Back: circular borzoi device. White endpapers. Top and bottom edges trimmed. Top edge stained purplish red.

Dust jacket: Front, spine, and back white with red and black overlapping bull's eyes. Front and back lettered in white on green rectangles. Signed: Bill English.

Publication: Published 11 April 1949. $2.50. Copyright #A31458.

Printing: Composed, printed, and bound by Kingsport Press, Kingsport, Tenn.

Locations: LC (APR 6 1949); Lilly (dj); MJB (dj).

Note: The first Lew Archer novel.

A 5.1.b
First edition, second printing. Boston: Gregg Press, 1979.

Introduction by Thomas Chastain. Ross Macdonald.

A 5.2
Second edition: New York: Knopf, 1949.

Mystery Guild. [i–vi] [1]–183 [184–186].

A 5.3
Third edition: New York: Pocket Books, [1950].

#680. Wrappers.

Dust jacket for A5.1.a

A 5.4
First English edition, only printing (1951)

THE MOVING TARGET

JOHN MACDONALD

CASSELL & COMPANY LTD
LONDON

A 5.4: $4^7/_8'' \times 7^1/_4''$

CASSELL & COMPANY LTD.
37-38 St. Andrews Hill
Queen Victoria Street
London E.C.4

and at

210 Queen Street, Melbourne
34 Clarence Street, Sydney
P.O. Box 9, Wellington, N.Z.
263-7 Adelaide Street, West Toronto
P.O. Box 275, Cape Town
P.O. Box 1386, Salisbury, S. Rhodesia
122 East 55th Street, New York
15 Graham Road, Ballard Estate, Bombay 1
Islands Brygge 5, Copenhagen
Gartenstrasse 53, Dusseldorf
Rua Maestro Elias Lobo 90, Sao Paulo
P.O. Box 959, Accra, Gold Coast

First published 1951

PRINTED IN GREAT BRITAIN BY
LOWE AND BRYDONE PRINTERS LTD. LONDON, N.W.10

[i–ii] [1–3] 4–245 [246]

[A]¹² B–H¹⁶

Contents: p. 1: half title; p. ii: '[fingerprint] A CRIME CONNOISSEUR | BOOK'; p. 1: title; p. 2: copyright; pp. 3–245: text; p. 246: blank.

Typography and paper: $5^{9}/_{16}''$ ($5^{13}/_{16}''$) × $3^{5}/_{8}''$. 31 lines per page. No running heads. Wove paper.

Binding: Black V-cloth (smooth). Spine silverstamped: '*THE* | *MOVING* | *TARGET* | [star] | *JOHN* | *MACDONALD* | [fingerprint] | *Crime* | *Connoisseur* | [rule] | *CASSELL*'. White endpapers. All edges trimmed.

Dust jacket: Front and spine art in shades of gray, red, green, and blue; back white. Front lettered in red, black, and white. Signed: J. Pollack.

Publication: 3,124 copies of the first printing. Published 14 November 1951. 10/6.

Printing: See copyright page.

Locations: BL (14 NOV 51), Lilly (dj), MJB (dj), UC-I (dj).

A5.5
Fifth edition: London: Pan Books, [1954].

#289. Wrappers. 39,200 copies. John Ross Macdonald.

A5.6.a
‚*Sixth edition:* New York: Pocket Books, [1959].

#2680. Wrappers. Reprinted as *Harper* by Ross Macdonald: New York: Pocket Books, [1966].

On copyright page: '4th printing . . . March, 1966'. #50218.

THE MOVING TARGET

A CRIME CONNOISSEUR BOOK

JOHN MACDONALD

CASSELL

Spine: THE MOVING TARGET — JOHN MACDONALD

The Sampson family made their money in the Texas oil fields, and spent it on the California coast. There was still plenty of it left when Ralph Sampson disappeared. Which is why Archer was called in by Mrs. Sampson, a paralysed blonde who had bad dreams, and by Albert Graves who held Sampson's power of attorney.

The trail that Archer followed took him down through the seven circles of California society. For Sampson had mixed with thieves and murderers, a cult of "sun-worshippers", a silent-movie star in the last stages of degradation and a bogus prophet who had saved her time. In company like that, kidnapping could be the least of anyone's trouble, and so Archer believed until he actually found Sampson and realised who was guilty.

But this was not before he had seen some plain and fancy evil, solved a series of violent crimes, and handed out some rough poetic justice.

10/6 net

Dust jacket for A5.4

A5.6.b
Sixth edition, Canadian printing: Harper. Richmond Hill, Ontario: Pocket Books of Canada, [1966].

On copyright page: '5th printing . . . March, 1966'.

50218. Wrappers. Ross Macdonald.

A5.7
Seventh edition: [London]: Collins/Fontana Books, [1966].

#1345. Wrappers. 36,688 copies. 4 printings, 1966–1978. Ross Macdonald.

A5.8
Eighth edition: Archer in Hollywood. New York: Knopf, 1967.

See AA 1.

A5.9
Ninth edition: New York, Toronto, London: Bantam, [1970].

#S5473. Wrappers. 10 printings, 1970–1977. Ross Macdonald.

A5.10.a
Tenth edition, first printing: South Yarmouth, Mass.: John Curley, [1979].†

Large-print edition. Wrappers. Ross Macdonald.

Note: The Moving Target is reported to be included in an unidentified two-volume mystery collection published by Readers Digest in England.

---

†Curley large-print editions are printed in Great Britain and distributed in cloth binding in the United Kingdom by Magna Print Books.

A6 THE DROWNING POOL

A6.1.a
First edition, first printing (1950)

JOHN ROSS
MACDONALD

THE

DROWNING

POOL

ALFRED A. KNOPF

 NEW YORK 1950

A6.1.a: 5³/₁₆″ × 7⁷/₁₆″

THIS IS A BORZOI BOOK,
PUBLISHED BY ALFRED A. KNOPF, INC.

[i–viii] [1–2] 3–244 [245–248]

$[1-8]^{16}$

Contents: p. i: blank; p. ii: card page; p. iii: blurb for *The Drowning Pool;* p. iv: blank; p. v.: title; p. vi: copyright; p. vii: 'TO TONY'; p. viii: blank; p. 1: half title; p. 2: blank: pp. 3–244: text; p. 245: blank; p. 246: note on type; pp. 247–248: blank.

Typography and paper: $5^{9}/_{16}''$ $(5^{13}/_{16}'')$ × 3 $^{11}/_{16}''$. 30 or 31 lines per page. Running heads: rectos and versos, '*THE DROWNING POOL*'. Wove paper.

Binding: Very pale green (#148) and brilliant green (#140) patterned paper-covered boards. Front: Blue and very very pale green rectangle with large fish swallowing small fish. Spine: '[in blue on very pale green panel] THE | DROWN- | -ING | POOL | *John* | *Ross* | *Macdonald* | KNOPF'. Back: Blue borzoi device on very pale green panel. White endpapers. Top and bottom edges trimmed. Top edge stained blue.

Dust jacket: Front and spine black; back black with blue panel across top. Front lettered in black on blue, with blue and white concentric circles. Signed: Bill English.

Publication: Published 21 August 1950. $2.50. Copyright #A 46937.

Printing: Composed, printed and bound by H. Wolff, New York.

Locations: LC (AUG 7 1950); Lilly (dj); MJB (dj); UC-I (dj).

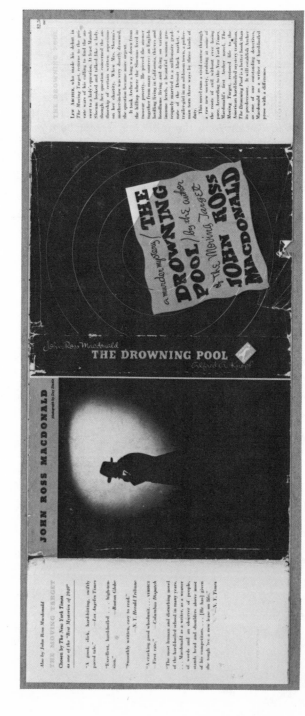

Dust jacket for A6.1.a

A 6.1.b
First edition, first English printing (1952)

THE DROWNING POOL

JOHN MACDONALD

CASSELL & COMPANY LTD
LONDON

A 6.1.b: $4^{13}/_{16}$" × $7^{1}/_{4}$"

CASSELL & COMPANY LTD.
37-38 St. Andrews Hill
Queen Victoria Street
London E.C.4

and at

210 Queen Street, Melbourne
26/30 Clarence Street, Sydney
P.O. Box 9, Wellington, N.Z.
263-7 Adelaide Street West, Toronto
P.O. Box 275, Cape Town
P.O. Box 1386, Salisbury, S. Rhodesia
122 East 55th Street, New York
15 Graham Road, Ballard Estate, Bombay 1
Islands Brygge 5, Copenhagen
Gartenstrasse 53, Dusseldorf
Avenida 9 de Julho 1138, Sao Paulo
P.O. Box 959, Accra, Gold Coast

First published 1952

PRINTED IN GREAT BRITAIN BY
LOWE AND BRYDONE (PRINTERS) LTD., LONDON, N.W.10

[i–x] [1–2] 3–244 [245–246]

[A]^{16} B–H^{16}

Contents: pp. i–ii: blank; p. iii: half title; p. iv: blank; p. v: blurb; p. vi: card page: '[fingerprint] A CRIME CONNOISSEUR | BOOK'; p. vii: title; p. viii: copyright; p. ix: dedication; p. x: blank; p. 1: half title; p. 2: blank; pp. 3–244: text; pp. 245–246: blank.

Typography and paper: Same as American first printing.

Binding: Black paper-covered boards with V-pattern (smooth). Spine silverstamped: 'THE | DROWNING | POOL | [star] | *John Macdonald* | [fingerprint] | *Crime* | *Connoisseur* | [rule] | CASSELL'. White endpapers. All edges trimmed.

Dust jacket: Front and spine in shades of blue and green; back white. Front lettered in white and greenish blue with yellow hat. Signed: Mudge-Marriott.

Publication: 3,754 copies of the first printing. Published 22 May 1952. 10/6.

Printing: See copyright page.

Locations: BL (1 MAY 52); MJB (dj); UC-I (dj).

A 6.1.c
First edition, third printing: New York & London: Garland, 1976.

Fifty Classics of Crime Fiction series. Ross Macdonald.

A 6.2
Second edition: New York: Pocket books, [1951].

#821. Wrappers. Second printing, 1959; third printing, 1966. John Ross Macdonald.

A 6.3
Third edition: London: Pan Books, 1955.

Wrappers. 34,407 copies. Not seen.

Dust jacket for A 6.1.b

A 6.4

Fourth edition: New York, London, Toronto: Bantam, [1970].

#S5472. Wrappers. 16 printings, 1970–1983. Ross Macdonald.

A 6.5

Fifth edition: [London]: Fontana/Collins, [1972].

#2975. Wrappers. Reprinted 1972, 1973, 1975. Ross Macdonald.

A 6.6

Sixth edition: South Yarmouth, Mass.: John Curley, [1979].

Large-print edition: Wrappers. Not seen.

A 7 THE WAY SOME PEOPLE DIE

A 7.1.a
First edition, first printing (1951)

John Ross Macdonald

THE

WAY

SOME

PEOPLE

DIE

New York *1951*

Alfred A. Knopf

A 7.1.a: 5^{1}/$_{8}$″ × 7^{1}/$_{2}$″

[i–viii] [1–3] 4–245 [246–248]

[1–8]^{16}

Contents: p. i: blank; p. ii: card page; p. iii: blurb for *The Way Some People Die;* p. iv: blank; p. v: title; p. vi: copyright; p. vii: '*To Roddy and Zella*'; p. viii: blank; p. 1: half title; p. 2: blank; pp. 3–245: text; p. 246: blank; p. 247: note on type; p. 248: blank.

Typography and paper: $5^3/4''$ ($5^{15}/_{16}''$) × $3^{11}/_{16}''$. 34 lines per page. Running heads: rectos and versos: '*THE WAY SOME PEOPLE DIE*'. Wove paper.

Binding: Brilliant blue (#177) and very pale blue (#184) patterned paper-covered boards. Spine: '[black on white panel] THE | *Way* | *Some* | *People* | *Die* | JOHN ROSS | MACDONALD | [on lower panel] ALFRED A. | KNOPF'. Back: borzoi seal on rectangular pale blue panel. White endpapers. Top and bottom edges trimmed. Top edge stained dark blue.

Dust jacket: Front and spine pink; back white. Front lettered in white, pink, and black with white art on black background.

Publication: Published 23 July 1951. $2.50. Copyright #A 56892.

Printing: Composed, printed, and bound by H. Wolff, New York.

Locations: LC (JUL 9 1951); Lilly (dj); MJB (dj).

A 7.1.b
First edition, second printing: New York: Knopf, 1951.

Not seen.

A 7.2.a
Second edition: New York: Pocket Books, [1952].

#907. Wrappers. Four printings, 1952–1967.

A 7.2.b
Second edition, Canadian printing: Reprinted in Canada by Pocket Books, 1953.

Wrappers. Not seen.

Dust jacket for A 7.1.a

A 7.3
First English edition, only printing (1953).

THE WAY
SOME PEOPLE DIE

JOHN ROSS MACDONALD

CASSELL & CO. LTD.
LONDON

A 7.3: $4^{15}/_{16}$" × $7^{1}/_{4}$"

CASSELL & CO. LTD.
37/38 St. Andrews Hill,
Queen Victoria Street,
London, E.C.4.
and at
210 Queen Street, Melbourne.
26/30 Clarence Street, Sydney.
P.O. Box 9, Lower Hutt, N.Z.
1068 Broadview Avenue, Toronto 6.
122 East 55th Street, New York 22.
Avenida 9 de Julho 1138, São Paulo.
Galeria Güemes, Escritorio 518/520 Florida 165, Buenos Aires.
Haroon Chambers, South Napier Road, Karachi.
15 Graham Road, Ballard Estate, Bombay, 1.
17 Central Avenue P.O. Dharamtala, Calcutta.
P.O. Box 275, Cape Town.
P.O. Box 1386, Salisbury, S. Rhodesia.
P.O. Box 959, Accra, Gold Coast.
Calcada Do Carma 55–20, Lisbon.
Klosterstrasse 34/36a, Düsseldorf.
25 rue Henri Barbusse, Paris 5e.
Islands Brygge 5, Copenhagen.

First published in Great Britain 1953

Set in 11 pt. Bembo type and
printed in Great Britain by
The Camelot Press Ltd., London and Southampton
F. 552

[1–6] 7–238 [239–240]

[A]^{16} B–F^{16} G^8 H^{16}

Contents: p. 1: half-title; p. 2: blurb, fingerprint, 'A CRIME CONNOISSEUR | BOOK'; p. 3: title; p. 4: copyright; p. 5: dedication; p. 6: blank; pp. 7–238: text; pp. 239–240: blank.

Typography and paper: 5⅝″ (5¹³/₁₆″) × 3¾″. 37 lines per page. No running heads. Wove paper.

Binding: Black paper-covered boards with V-pattern. Sprine silverstamped: 'THE WAY | SOME | PEOPLE | DIE | [star] | John Ross | Macdonald | [fingerprint] | Crime | Connoisseur | [rule] | CASSELL'. White endpapers. All edges trimmed.

Dust jacket: Front and spine lettered in yellow, orange, pale blue, and maroon; signed: 'MUDGE-MARRIOTT'.

Publication: 3,731 copies of the first printing. Published 14 May 1953. 10/6.

Printing: See copyright page.

Locations: BL (8 MAY 53); UC-I (dj), MJB.

Publication of *The Way Some People Die* in America produced in the *New York Times* the ecstatic comment: "after many long years a worthy successor to Dashiell Hammett". Two fast, hard-hitting thrillers by John Ross Macdonald, *The Moving Target* and *The Drowning Pool* have already been published. This latest story confirms our belief that Macdonald is on top of all rivals in this special field of detective literature.

This is the story of Galley, a young woman who was not so nice as her mother thought her, and of Archer who, delegated to find her, finds also a viper's nest. Galley has a soft body and a hard heart but neither prevents Archer from sorting out the mess into which a love of men and money has dragged her not unwilling feet.

10s. 6d. net.

THE WAY SOME PEOPLE DIE

JOHN ROSS MACDONALD

A CRIME CONNOISSEUR BOOK

THE WAY SOME PEOPLE DIE

JOHN ROSS MACDONALD

CASSELL CRIME CONNOISSEUR BOOK

CASSELL MYSTERIES

Dust jacket for A 7.3

A 7.4

Fourth edition: London: Pan. [1956].

#370. Wrappers. 40,500 copies.

A 7.5

Fifth edition: Archer in Hollywood. New York: Knopf, 1967.

Includes *The Way Some People Die.* See AA1.

A 7.6

Sixth edition: New York, Toronto, London: Bantam, [1971].

#N6747. Wrappers. 6 printings. Ross Macdonald. p. i: ' " Some of my colleagues think that THE WAY SOME PEOPLE DIE is the best of my twenty books.'—Ross Macdonald."

A 7.7

Seventh edition: London: Fontana/Collins, [1973].

#3176. Wrappers.

A 7.8

Eighth edition: [London]: Severn House, [1977].

Ross Macdonald.

A 7.9

Ninth edition: South Yarmouth, Mass.: John Curley, [1980].

Large-print edition. Wrappers. Ross Macdonald.

A 8 THE IVORY GRIN

A 8.1.a
First edition, first printing (1952)

John Ross Macdonald

THE

IVORY

GRIN

1952

Alfred A. Knopf: New York

A 8.1.a: $5^3/_{16}$" × $7^1/_2$"

L. C. catalog card number: 51–13221

⚘ THIS IS A BORZOI BOOK,
PUBLISHED BY ALFRED A. KNOPF, INC. ⚘

Copyright 1952 by Alfred A. Knopf, Inc. All rights reserved. No part of this book may be reproduced in any form without permission in writing from the publisher, except by a reviewer who may quote brief passages in a review to be printed in a magazine or newspaper. Manufactured in the United States of America. Published simultaneously in Canada by McClelland & Stewart Limited.

FIRST EDITION

[i–x] [i–2] 3–240 [241–246]

[1–8]^{16}

Contents: p. i–iii: blank; p. iv: card page; p. v: blurb for *The Ivory Grin;* p. vi: blank; p. vii: title; p. viii: copyright; p. ix: ' *'To all HANDS'*; p. x: blank; p. 1: half title; p. 2: blank; pp. 3–240: text; p. 241: blank; p. 242: note on type; pp. 243–246: blank.

Typography and paper: 5^{1}/$_{2}$″ (5^{3}/$_{4}$″) × 3^{11}/$_{16}$″. 32 or 33 lines per page. Running heads: rectos and versos, *''THE IVORY GRIN'*. Wove paper.

Binding: Strong reddish orange (#35) and pale yellowish pink (#31) paper-covered boards. Spine: [black on white panel] *The | Ivory | Grin* | JOHN ROSS | MACDONALD | [on lower panel] ALFRED A. | KNOPF'. Back: black borzoi device on pale yellowish pink panel. White endpapers. Top edge trimmed and stained dark gray.

Dust jacket: Front and spine black; back white with red panels. Front lettered in red, white, and green with title in white on 3 red panels. Signed: Hoffman.

Publication: Published 5 May 1952. $2.50. Copyright #A 65961.

Printing: Composed, printed, and bound by H. Wolff, New York.

Locations: LC (APR 21 1952); Lilly (dj); MJB (dj).

A 8.1.b
First edition, second printing: New York: Knopf, 1952.

On copyright page: 'SECOND PRINTING, MAY 1952'.

Dust jacket for A 8.1.a

A 8.2
First English edition, only printing (1953)

THE IVORY GRIN

by

JOHN ROSS MACDONALD

CASSELL & COMPANY LTD.

LONDON

A 8.2: $4^7/_8'' \times 7^1/_4''$

CASSELL & CO. LTD.
37/38 St. Andrew's Hill, Queen Victoria Street,
London, E.C.4.

and at

210 Queen Street, Melbourne.
26/30 Clarence Street, Sydney.
Haddon Hall, City Road, Auckland, N.Z.
1068 Broadview Avenue, Toronto 6.
122 East 55th Street, New York 22.
Avenida 9 de Julho 1138, São Paulo.
Galeria Güemes, Escritorio 518/520 Florida 165, Buenos Aires.
Haroon Chambers, South Napier Road, Karachi.
15 Graham Road, Ballard Estate, Bombay, 1.
17 Central Avenue P.O., Dharamtala, Calcutta.
P.O. Box 275, Cape Town.
P.O. Box 1386, Salisbury, S. Rhodesia.
P.O. Box 959, Accra, Gold Coast.
Calçada Do Carma, 55-2⁰, Lisbon.
25 rue Henri Barbusse, Paris, 5e.
Islands Brygge 5, Copenhagen.

First published in Great Britain 1953

*Set in 12 pt. Bembo type and
printed in Great Britain by
The Camelot Press Ltd., London and Southampton*
F.653

[1–6] 7–255 [256]

[A]^{16} B–H^{16}

Contents: p. 1: half title; p. 2: blurb, other books by Macdonald, [fingerprint] 'A CRIME CONNOISSEUR | BOOK'; p. 3: title; p. 4: copyright; p. 5: dedication; p. 6: blank; pp. 7–255: text; p. 256: blank.

Typography and paper: 5^{13}/₁₆″ (6^{1}/₁₆″) × 3^{9}/₁₆″. 35 lines per page. No running heads. Wove paper.

Binding: Black paper-covered boards with V-pattern (smooth). Spine silverstamped: '*THE* | *IVORY* | *GRIN* | [star] | *John Ross* | *Macdonald* | [fingerprint] | *Crime* | *Connoisseur* | [rule] | *CASSELL*'. White endpapers. All edges trimmed.

Dust jacket: Front and spine green; back white. Front lettered in red and white with white skull. Signed: Mudge-Marriott.

Publication: 3,984 copies of the first printing. Published 22 October 1953. 10/6.

Printing: See copyright page.

Locations: BL (9 OCT 53); MJB (dj); UC-I (dj).

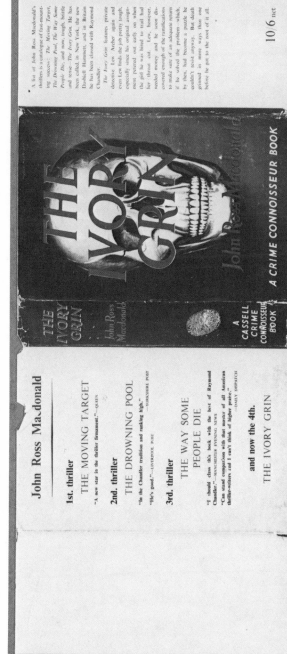

Dust jacket for A 8.2

A 8.3
Third edition: Marked for Murder. New York: Pocket Books, [1953].

#971. Wrappers. 3 printings, 1953–1967; third printing as *The Ivory Grin* by Ross Macdonald.

A 8.4
Fourth edition: London: Pan, [1957].

#410. Wrappers. 65,645 copies.

A 8.5
Fifth edition: [London]: Collins/Fontana Books, [1965].

#2029. Wrappers. 27,065 copies. Reprinted 1970, 1971, 1973, 1976. Ross Macdonald.

A 8.6
Sixth edition: New York, Toronto, London: Bantam, [1971].

#N6774. Wrappers. 6 printings, 1971–1977. Ross Macdonald.

A 8.7
Seventh edition: South Yarmouth, Mass.: John Curley, [1981].

Large-print edition. Wrappers. Not seen.

A 9 MEET ME AT THE MORGUE

A 9.1.a
First edition, first printing (1953)

John Ross Macdonald

MEET ME

AT THE

MORGUE

 1953

Alfred A. Knopf: New York

A 9.1.a: 5³/₁₆″ × 7⁷/₁₆″

L. C. *catalog card number:* 52–12208

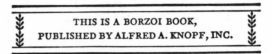

THIS IS A BORZOI BOOK,
PUBLISHED BY ALFRED A. KNOPF, INC.

Copyright 1953 by Alfred A. Knopf, Inc. All rights reserved. No part of this book may be reproduced in any form without permission in writing from the publisher, except by a reviewer who may quote brief passages in a review to be printed in a magazine or newspaper. Manufactured in the United States of America. Published simultaneously in Canada by McClelland & Stewart Limited.

FIRST EDITION

A condensed version of this novel appeared in *Cosmopolitan* under the title *Experience with Evil.*

[i–viii] [1–2] 3–212 [213–216]

[1–7]^{16}

Contents: p. i: blank; p. ii: card page; p. iii: blurb for *Meet Me at the Morgue;* p. iv: blank; p. v.: title; p. vi: copyright; p. vii: '*TO MY FAVORITE IN-LAWS | DOROTHY & CLARENCE*'; p. viii: blank; p. 1: half title; p. 2: blank; pp. 3–212: text; p. 213: blank; p. 214: note on type; pp. 215–216: blank.

Typography and paper: 5^{11}/₁₆″ (5^{15}/₁₆″) × 3^{11}/₁₆″. 34 lines per page. Running heads: rectos and versos: '*MEET ME AT THE MORGUE*'. Wove paper.

Binding: Strong orange yellow (#68) and light orange yellow (#70) patterned paper-covered boards. Spine: '[in black on white panel] *Meet | Me | at the | Morgue* | [decoration] | JOHN ROSS | MACDONALD | [on lower panel] ALFRED A. | KNOPF'. Back: black borzoi device on light orange yellow panel. White end papers. Top and bottom edges trimmed. Top edge stained blue. Also noted with top edge unstained.

Dust jacket: Front and spine gray; back white. Front lettered in white and black with white, red, and black art. Signed: English.

Publication: Published 18 May 1953. $2.50. Copyright #A 88307.

Printing: Composed, printed, and bound by H. Wolff, New York.

Locations: LC (t.e. stained, APR 24 1953); Lilly (t.e. stained, dj); MJB (t.e. stained, dj); ScU (t.e. unstained); UC-I (t.e. stained, dj).

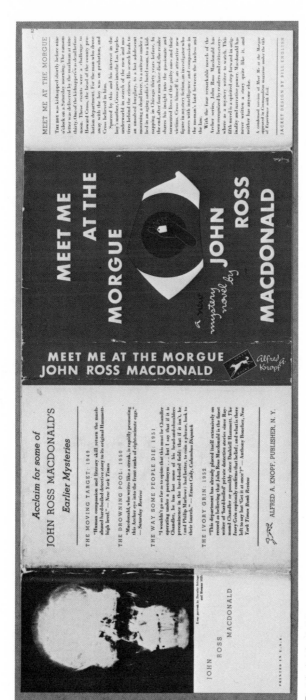

Dust jacket for A 9.1.a

A 9.1.b
First edition, second printing: New York: Knopf, [1953].

Mystery Guild.

A 9.2
First English edition, only printing (1954)

EXPERIENCE WITH EVIL

by

JOHN ROSS MACDONALD

CASSELL & COMPANY LTD

LONDON

A 9.2: $4^7/_8'' \times 7^1/_2''$

CASSELL & CO. LTD.
37/38 St. Andrew's Hill,
Queen Victoria Street,
London, E.C.4.

and at

31/34 George IV Bridge, Edinburgh.
210 Queen Street, Melbourne.
26/30 Clarence Street, Sydney.
Haddon Hall, City Road, Auckland, N.Z.
1068 Broadview Avenue, Toronto 6.
420 West 45th Street, New York 36.
Avenida 9 de Julho 1138, São Paulo.
Galeria Güemes, Escritorio 518/520 Florida 165, Buenos Aires.
Haroon Chambers, South Napier Road, Karachi.
15 Graham Road, Ballard Estate, Bombay, 1.
17 Central Avenue P.O., Dharamtala, Calcutta.
P.O. Box 275, Cape Town.
P.O. Box 1386, Salisbury, S. Rhodesia.
P.O. Box 959, Accra, Gold Coast.
25 rue Henri Barbusse, Paris, 5e.
Islands Brygge 5, Copenhagen.

First published in Great Britain 1954

Set in 11pt. Bembo type and
printed in Great Britain by
The Camelot Press Ltd., London and Southampton
F.1153

[1–6] 7–200

[A]⁸ B–I⁸ K–L⁸ M⁴ N⁸

Contents: p. 1: half title; p. 2: blurb for *Experience with Evil,* books by Macdonald, fingerprint, 'A CRIME CONNOISSEUR | BOOK'; p. 3: title; p. 4: copyright; p. 5: dedication; p. 6: blank; pp. 7–200: text.

Typography and paper: 5⅝″ (5⅞″) × 3¹¹/₁₆″. 37 lines per page. No running heads. Wove paper.

Binding: Black paper-covered boards with V-pattern (smooth). Spine goldstamped: 'EXPERIENCE | WITH | EVIL | [star] | *John Ross* | *Macdonald* | [fingerprint] | *Crime* | *Connoisseur* | [rule] | *CASSELL*'. White endpapers. All edges trimmed.

Dust jacket: Front predominantly blue and brown; spine black; back white. Front lettered in white, red, and yellow. Signed: Mudge-Marriott.

Publication: 5,946 copies of the first printing. Published 8 April 1954. 10/6.

Printing: See copyright page.

Locations: BL (22 MAR 54); MJB (dj); UC-I (dj).

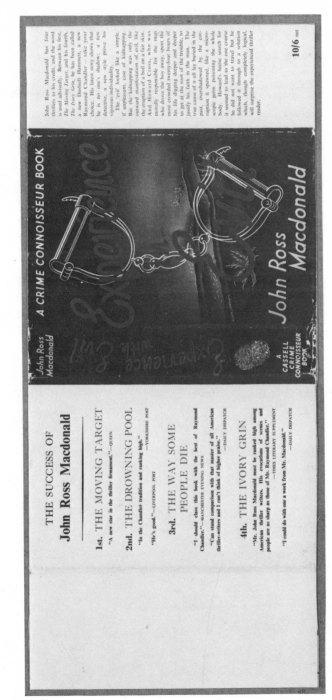

Dust jacket for A 9.2

A 9.3.a
Third edition: New York: Pocket Books, [1954].

#1020. Wrappers. 4 printings, 1954–1967.

A 9.3.b
Third edition, Canadian printing: Reprinted in Canada by Pocket Books, 1955.

Wrappers. Not seen.

A 9.4
Fourth edition: Experience with Evil. London: Pan, [1958].

#G104. Wrappers. 50,013 copies.

A 9.5.a
Fifth edition: New York, Toronto, London: Bantam, [1972].

#N7344. Wrappers. 4 printings, 1972–1980. Ross Macdonald.

A 9.5.b
Fifth edition, Candian printing: New York, Toronto, London: Bantam, [1980].

On copyright page: '4th printing . . . January 1980'. Wrappers. Ross Macdonald

Note 1: Condensed as "Experience with Evil," *Cosmopolitan* 134 (March 1953), 129–154.

Note 2: A 1954 Australian serialization has been reported. Not seen.

A 10 FIND A VICTIM

A 10.1
First edition, only printing (1954)

$\mathbf{F}_{ind}$ a $\mathbf{V}_{ictim}$

John Ross Macdonald

New York: Alfred A. Knopf: 1954

A 10.1: 5^1/$_8$″ × 7^7/$_{16}$″

L. C. catalog card number: 53–9478

THIS IS A BORZOI BOOK,
PUBLISHED BY ALFRED A. KNOPF, INC.

FIRST EDITION

[i–viii] [1–2] 3–215 [216]

[1–7]^{16}

Contents: p. i: blank; p. ii: card page; p. iii: blurb for *Find a Victim;* p. iv: 3-line epigraph from Stephen Crane; p. v: title; p. vi: copyright; p. vii: 'To *Ivan von Auw, Jr.*'; p. viii: blank; p. 1: half title; p. 2: blank; pp. 3–215: text; p. 216: note on type.

Typography and paper: 5¾″ (6¹/₁₆″) × 3⁵/₈″. 34 or 35 lines per page. Running heads: rectos and versos, *'FIND A VICTIM'.* Wove paper.

Binding: Medium reddish brown (#43) and medium yellowish pink (#29) patterned paper-covered boards. Spine: '[in black on white panel] *Find | A | Victim* | [rosette] | JOHN ROSS | MACDONALD | [on lower panel] ALFRED A. | KNOPF'. Back has black borzoi device on medium yellowish pink panel. White endpapers. Top and bottom edges trimmed. Top edge stained greenish blue.

Dust jacket: Front, spine, and back white. Front lettered in red with black-and-white photo of footprint. 3 black-and-white photos of Macdonald on back.

Publication: Published 26 July 1954. $2.75. Copyright #A 142742.

Printing: Composed, printed, and bound by H. Wolff, New York.

Locations: LC (JUN 25 1954); Lilly (dj); MJB (dj); UC-I (dj).

Dust jacket for A 10.1

A 10.2
First English edition, only printing (1955)

FIND A VICTIM

by

JOHN ROSS MACDONALD

CASSELL & COMPANY LTD

LONDON

A 10.2: $4^{13}/_{16}$″ × $7^{3}/_{16}$″

CASSELL & CO. LTD.
37/38 St. Andrew's Hill, Queen Victoria Street,
London, E.C.4.

and at

31/34 George IV Bridge, Edinburgh.
210 Queen Street, Melbourne.
26/30 Clarence Street, Sydney.
Haddon Hall, City Road, Auckland, N.Z.
1068 Broadview Avenue, Toronto 6.
P.O. Box 275, Cape Town.
P.O. Box 1386, Salisbury, S. Rhodesia.
Haroon Chambers, South Napier Road, Karachi.
Munshi Niketan, behind Kamla Market, Ajmeri Gate, Delhi.
15 Graham Road, Ballard Estate, Bombay, 1.
17 Central Avenue P.O., Dharamtala, Calcutta.
122 East 55th Street, New York 22.
Avenida 9 de Julho 1138, São Paulo.
Galeria Güemes, Escritorio 518/520 Florida 165, Buenos Aires.
P.O. Box 959, Accra, Gold Goast.
25 rue Henri Barbusse, Paris, 5e.
Islands Brygge 5, Copenhagen.

First published 1955

*Set in 11 pt. Bembo type and
printed in Great Britain by
The Camelot Press Ltd., London and Southampton*
F.854

[1–4] 5–208

[A]⁸ B–I⁸ K–N⁸

Contents: p.1: blurb for *Find a Victim;* p. 2: card page, fingerprint, 'A CRIME CON-NOISSEUR | BOOK'; p. 3: title; p. 4: copyright; pp. 5–208: text.

Typography and paper: $5^3/4''$ (6") $\times 3^{11}/_{16}''$. 38 lines per page. No running heads. Wove paper.

Binding: Black paper-covered boards with V-pattern (smooth). Spine silverstamped: '*FIND A* | *VICTIM* | [star] | *John Ross* | *Macdonald* | [fingerprint] | *Crime* | *Connoisseur* | [rule] | *CASSELL*'. White endpapers. All edges trimmed.

Dust jacket: Front and spine art in blue, yellow, and brown; back white. Front lettered in blue, white, and red.

Publication: 6,839 copies of the first printing. Published 27 January 1955. 9/6.

Printing: See copyright page.

Location: MJB (dj).

Dust jacket for A 10.2

A 10.4
Fourth edition: London: Pan [1958].

#G146. Wrappers. 44,172 copies.

A 10.5
Fifth edition: New York: Bantam, [1962].

Copyright #A2388. Wrappers. Reprinted 1967. Ross Macdonald. Distributed in England by Transworld Corgi in 1964; not seen.

A 10.6
Sixth edition: [London]: Fontana/Collins, [1971].

#2630. Wrappers. Ross Macdonald. 5 printings, 1971–1975.

A 10.7.a
Seventh edition, first printing: New York, Toronto, London: Bantam, [1972].

#N7432. Wrappers. Reprinted. Ross Macdonald.

A 10.7.b
Seventh edition, Canadian printings: New York, Toronto, London: Bantam, [1979].

On copyright page: '4th printing . . . November 1979'.

Wrappers. Reprinted 1980. Ross Macdonald.

A 10.8
Eighth edition: [London]: Severn House, [1976].

Ross Macdonald.

Note: Condensed in *Manhunt* 2 (July 1954), 90–141. Reissued in *Giant Manhunt*, no. 4.

A 11 THE NAME IS ARCHER

A 11.1.a
First edition, first printing (1955)

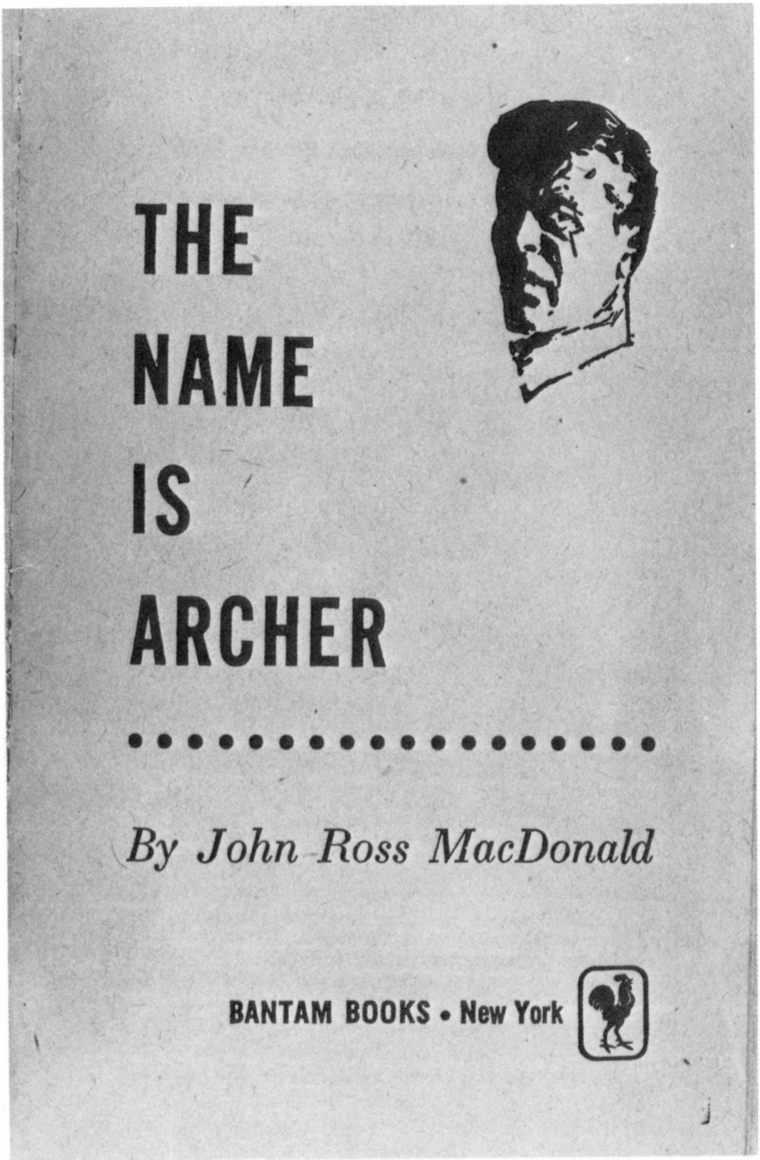

THE

NAME

IS

ARCHER

• • • • • • • • • • • • • • • • • •

By John Ross MacDonald

BANTAM BOOKS • New York

A 11.1.a: $4^3/_{16}'' \times 7''$

THE NAME IS ARCHER

A BANTAM BOOK published February 1955

Copyright, 1946, 1948, 1953, 1954 by Kenneth Millar

Copyright, 1955 by Kenneth Millar

Bantam Books are published by Bantam Books, Inc. Its
trade mark, consisting of the words "BANTAM BOOKS"
and the portrayal of a bantam, is registered in the U. S.
Patent Office and in other countries. *Marca Registrada*

PRINTED IN THE UNITED STATES OF AMERICA

BANTAM BOOKS, 25 West 45th Street, New York 36, New York

[i–vi] 1–194

Perfect binding. Unsigned.

Contents: p. i: blurb; p. ii: blank; p. iii: title; p. iv: copyright; p. v: contents; p. vi: blank;
pp. 1–194: text.

7 stories: "Find the Woman" (C 55), "Gone Girl" (C 61),† "The Bearded Lady"
(C 57),† "The Suicide" (C 64),† "Guilt-Edged Blonde" (C 66),† "The Sinister Habit"
(C 63),† "Wild Goose Chase" (C 67). Daggers indicate first book publication. "The
Bearded Lady" and "Find the Woman" were rewritten as Lew Archer stories for this
collection. See C 55, C 57.

Typography and paper: $6^{1}/_{16}''$ ($6^{5}/_{16}''$) × $3^{7}/_{8}''$. Running heads: rectos, story title; versos, 'THE NAME IS ARCHER'. Wove paper.

Binding: Printed paper wrappers. Front printed in black, white, and brown-red against
yellow-green background; torso of man with revolver and other figures. Spine printed in
white and red against black. Back printed in black, blue, and red. All edges trimmed.

Publication: 25¢. #1295.

Printing: Unknown.

Locations: Lilly; MJB; UC-I.

A 11.1.b
First edition, second printing: New York: Bantam, 1955.

Wrappers. Not seen.

A 11.1.c
First edition, third printing: New York, Toronto, London: Bantam, [1966].

#F3132. Wrappers. Ross Macdonald.

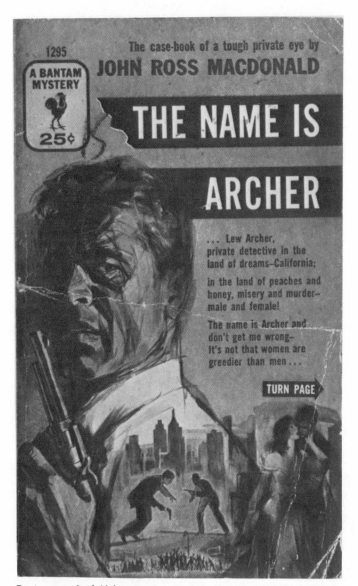

The case-book of a tough private eye by
JOHN ROSS MACDONALD

1295

A BANTAM MYSTERY

25¢

THE NAME IS
ARCHER

. . . Lew Archer,
private detective in the
land of dreams—California;

in the land of peaches and
honey, misery and murder—
male and female!

The name is Archer and
don't get me wrong—
It's not that women are
greedier than men . . .

TURN PAGE

Front wrapper for A 11.1.a

A 11.1.d

First edition, Canadian printing: New York, Toronto, London: Bantam, [1966].

On copyright page: '3rd printing . . . May 1966'.

#F3132. Wrappers. Ross Macdonald.

A 11.1.e

First edition, fourth printing: New York: Bantam, 1966.

Wrappers. Not seen.

A 11.2

Second edition: New York, Toronto, London: Bantam, [1971].

#N5996. Wrappers. 10 printings, 1971–1979. Ross Macdonald.

A 11.3
First English edition, only printing (1976)

ROSS MACDONALD

The Name is Archer

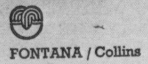

FONTANA / Collins

A 11.3: 4³/₁₆″ × 7¹/₁₆″

[1–6] 7–190 [191–192]

Perfect Binding.

Contents: p.1: blurb; p. 2: card page; p. 3: title; p. 4: copyright; p. 5: contents; p. 6: blank; pp. 7–190: text; pp. 191–192: ads.

6 stories: "Find the Woman," "Gone Girl," "The Bearded Lady," "The Suicide," "Guilt-Edged Blonde," "Wild Goose Chase."

Typography and paper: 5³/₄″ (6³/₁₆″) × 3¹/₂″. 41 or 42 lines per page. Running heads: rectos, story title; versos, 'THE NAME IS ARCHER'. Wove paper.

Binding: Wrappers. Photo of wallet with coins, cigarette pack and pencil across front spine and back. Lettered in black and red against white. All edges trimmed.

Publication: Published in May 1976. 50 pp. #4219.

Printing: See copyright page.

Location: MJB.

Front wrapper for A 11.3

A 12 THE BARBAROUS COAST

A 12.1
First edition, only printing (1956)

The Barbarous Coast

by Ross Macdonald

Alfred A. Knopf : N E W   Y O R K : *1956*

A 12.1.: 5^1/$_8$″ × 7^1/$_2$″

L.C. catalog card number: 56–6507

© Ross Macdonald, 1956

THIS IS A BORZOI BOOK,
PUBLISHED BY ALFRED A. KNOPF, INC.

FIRST EDITION

A condensed version of this novel appeared in
Cosmopolitan under the title of THE DYING ANIMAL

[i–viii] [1–3] 4–247 [248]

[1–8]¹⁶

Contents: p. i: blank; p. ii: card page, 7 titles; p. iii: blurb for *The Barbarous Coast;* p. iv: 3 lines of type decoration; p. v: title; p. vi: copyright; p. vii: 'FOR STANLEY TENNY'; p. viii: disclaimer; p. 1: half title; p. 2: blank; pp. 3–247: text; p. 248: note on type.

Paper and typography: 5⁷/₈″ (6¹/₁₆″) × 3¹¹/₁₆″. 34 or 35 lines per page. Running heads: versos only, 'THE BARBAROUS COAST'. Wove paper.

Binding: Strong reddish orange (#35) and pale yellowish pink (#31) paper-covered boards. Spine: '[in black on white panel] THE *Bar- | barous | Coast* | [decoration] | ROSS | MACDONALD | [on lower panel] ALFRED A. | KNOPF'. Back has black borzoi device on pale yellowish pink rectangle. White endpapers. Top and bottom edges trimmed. Top edge stained greenish blue.

Dust jacket: Front and spine greenish blue and yellow; back white. Front lettered in black with drawing of woman in white and greenish blue.

Publication: Published 18 June 1956. $2.95. Copyright #A 236636.

Printing: Composed, printed, and bound by H. Wolff, New York.

Locations: LC (MAY 23 1956); Lilly (dj); MJB (dj); UC-I (dj).

Dust jacket for A 12.1

A 12.2
First English edition, only printing (1957)

THE BARBAROUS COAST

by

JOHN ROSS MACDONALD

CASSELL & COMPANY LTD
LONDON

A 12.2: $4^{13}/_{16}'' \times 7^{3}/_{16}''$

```
┌─────────────────────────────────────────────────────────────┐
│                   CASSELL & CO LTD                           │
│                 37/38 St. Andrew's Hill,                     │
│                   Queen Victoria Street,                     │
│                     London, E.C.4                           │
│                                                             │
│                        and at                               │
│                                                             │
│              31/34 George IV Bridge, Edinburgh              │
│                210 Queen Street, Melbourne                  │
│                26/30 Clarence Street, Sydney                │
│          24 Wyndham Street, Auckland, New Zealand           │
│             1068 Broadview Avenue, Toronto 6                │
│                 P.O. Box 275, Cape Town                     │
│                P.O. Box 11190, Johannesburg                 │
│              P.O. Box 189, Bridgetown, Barbados             │
│            13/14 Ajmeri Gate Extension, New Delhi 1         │
│           15 Graham Road, Ballard Estate, Bombay 1          │
│              17 Chittaranjan Avenue, Calcutta 13            │
│        Macdonald House, Orchard Road, Singapore 9           │
│               P.O. Box 959, Accra, Gold Coast               │
│              Avenida 9 de Julho 1138, São Paulo             │
│   Galeria Güemes, Escritorio 454/59 Florida 165, Buenos Aires │
│                 Marne 5b, Mexico 5, D.F.                    │
│               25 rue Henri Barbusse, Paris 5e               │
│            25 Ny Strandvej, Espergaerde, Denmark            │
│                 Kauwlaan 17, The Hague                      │
│                                                             │
│                                                             │
│          First published in Great Britain 1957             │
│                  All rights reserved                        │
│                                                             │
│                Set in 11-pt Bembo type and                  │
│                printed in Great Britain by                  │
│       Wyman and Sons Ltd., London, Reading and Fakenham     │
│                        F.1156                               │
└─────────────────────────────────────────────────────────────┘
```

[1–6] 7–240

[A] B–I K–P⁸

Contents: p. 1: half title; p. 2: blurb, other books by JRM, fingerprint, 'A CRIME CONNOISSEUR | BOOK'; p. 3: title; p. 4: copyright; p. 5: dedication; p. 6: blank; pp. 7–240: text.

Typography and paper: $5^5/8''$ $(5^7/8'')$ × $3^5/8''$. 37 lines per page. No running heads. Wove paper.

Binding: Black paper-covered boards with V-pattern. Spine silverstamped: 'THE | BARBAROUS | COAST | [star] | John Ross | Macdonald | [fingerprint] | CRIME | CON-NOISSEUR | [rule] | CASSELL'. White endpapers. All edges trimmed; top edge unstained. Also deep blue (#179) V-cloth (smooth) with spine silverstamped: 'THE | BARBAROUS | COAST | JOHN ROSS | MACDONALD | *Cassell*'. Top edge stained yellow.

Dust jacket: Front and spine lettered in yellow, red, and white against blue background.

Though Lew Archer was called to the exclusive beach-side Channel Club in Malibu to save the club manager from a dangerously angry husband, he soon discovered that the club swimming pool was the depository for a lot of dirty linen. The angry young husband's wife, Hester, had recently been an exhibition diver at the pool; now she was missing. Two years before, her eighteen-year-old predecessor, Gabrielle, had been found dead early one morning on the adjoining beach.

Looking for Hester, Lew Archer found the mystery of Gabrielle's death constantly obtruding. He also found himself up against a number of unpleasant characters who disliked his interest in both the missing girl and the dead one. Fast, tough and exciting, this story is John Ross Macdonald at his punch-packed best; if you read mysteries as a sedative, keep away from this one.

11'6 NET

THE BARBAROUS COAST

John Ross Macdonald

A
CASSELL
CRIME
CONNOISSEUR
BOOK

A CRIME CONNOISSEUR BOOK

Dust jacket for A 12.2

Publication: 6,054 copies of the first printing. Published 25 April 1957. 11/6.

Printing: See copyright page.

Locations: BL (black, 9 MAR 57); MJB (black and blue); UC-I (black; dj).

A 12.3.a
Third edition, first printing: New York: Bantam, 1957.

#1613. Wrappers. Not seen. 7 printings, 1957–1979.

A 12.3.b
Third edition, Canadian printing: New York, Toronto, London: Bantam, [1979].

#12249-5. Wrappers. Canadian printings in 1957 and 1966 reported but not seen.

A 12.4
Fourth edition: London: Pan, [1959].

#G260. Wrappers. 40,392 copies.

A 12.5
Fifth edition: [London]: Collins/Fontana, [1967].

#1547. Wrappers. 20,866 copies. Reprinted 1972.

A 12.6
Sixth edition: Archer in Hollywood. New York: Knopf, 1967.

Includes *The Barbarous Coast.* See AA 1.

A 12.7
Seventh edition: South Yarmouth, Mass.: John Curley, [1979].

Large-print edition. Wrappers.

Note 1: *The Barbarous Coast* was the first volume published as by Ross Macdonald.

Note 2: Condensed as "The Dying Animal," *Cosmopolitan* 140 (March 1956), 84–111.

A 13 THE DOOMSTERS

A 13.1
First edition, only printing (1958)

THE
DOOMSTERS

Ross Macdonald

ALFRED A. KNOPF   *New York*   1958

A 13.1: 5¹/8″ × 7⁷/16″

Purissima is an imaginary city. The people who "live" in and around it are imaginary. No reference to actual people or places is intended.

L. C. Catalog card number: 58–5829
© Ross Macdonald, 1958

THIS IS A BORZOI BOOK,
PUBLISHED BY ALFRED A. KNOPF, INC.

Copyright 1958 by Ross Macdonald. All rights reserved. No part of this book may be reproduced in any form without permission in writing from the publisher, except by a reviewer who may quote brief passages in a review to be printed in a magazine or newspaper. Manufactured in the United States of America. Published simultaneously in Canada by McClelland & Stewart Ltd.

FIRST EDITION

The lines quoted on page 225 are from "To an Unborn Pauper Child" and are reprinted with the permission of The Macmillan Company from *Collected Poems of Thomas Hardy.*

[i–iv] [1–3] 4–251 [252]

[1–8]^{16}

Contents: p. i: blurb for *The Doomsters;* p. ii: card page, 8 titles; p. iii: title; p. iv: copyright; p. 1: 'THE DOOMSTERS | *For John and Dick, Hill-climbers';* p. 2: blank; pp. 3–251: text; p. 252: note on author and note on type.

Typography and paper: 5^{13}/$_{16}$" (6") × 3^{11}/$_{16}$". 34 lines per page. Running heads: versos only, 'THE DOOMSTERS'. Wove paper.

Binding: Strong reddish purple (#237) and pale purplish pink (#252) patterned paper-covered boards. Spine: '[black on white panel] THE | *Doom-* | *sters* | [rosette] | Ross | Macdonald | [on lower panel] ALFRED A. | KNOPF'. Back cover has black borzoi device on rectangular pale purplish pink panel. White endpapers. Top and bottom edges trimmed. Top edge stained very pale orange.

Dust jacket: Front and spine black; back white. Front lettered in white and blue, with orange, brown, and blue figures.

Publication: Published 17 February 1958. $2.95. Copyright #A319902.

Printing: Composed, printed, and bound by H. Wolff, New York.

Locations: LC (JAN 21 1958); Lilly (dj); MJB (dj); UC-I(dj).

THE DOOMSTERS

Ross Macdonald
THE DOOMSTERS
Alfred A. Knopf

Ross Macdonald

What reviewers have said about earlier MACDONALD books:

THE BARBAROUS COAST (1956)
"An admirable, thoroughly absorbing piece of work."
—*New York Herald Tribune*

FIND A VICTIM (1954)
"It seems to belong to a ... genre of its own."
—*The New York Times*

MEET ME AT THE MORGUE (1953)
"Characters in the round, believable evil and charity of telling make another fine Macdonald story."
—Lenore Glen Offord, *San Francisco Chronicle*

THE IVORY GRIN (1952)
"The finest writer of hard-boiled private detective stories since Raymond Chandler or possibly since Dashiell Hammett."
—Anthony Boucher, *The New York Times Book Review*

BORZOI BOOKS
ALFRED A KNOPF PUBLISHER

Photograph by Olive Carlton

ROSS MACDONALD
—i.e. Kenneth Millar—was born in California in 1915 of Canadian-American ancestry. He was educated in Canada, and in 1938 married a Canadian girl who is now well known as a novelist under her married name, Margaret Millar. After several years of high-school teaching, he was given a fellowship at the University of Michigan and took his Ph.D. in American literature, with a study of Coleridge's psychology. He entered the Navy in 1944 and served as a communications officer on an escort carrier. For some years he has been writing mystery novels under the name John Ross Macdonald but in 1956, for fear of possible confusion with John D. MacDonald changed his pen name to Ross Macdonald. The Doomsters is his thirteenth published book.

When Archer opened the door to the tall young man who was afraid of the light, he was letting the Doomsters in.

What were the Doomsters?

The well-to-do woman who drank too much: she told the tale, knew them.

So did the aging juvenile delinquent who used drugs to dull a nightmare memory.

So did Carl, who was running away from a certain place and a certain thing, and who might have found his way back if only he could have caught himself on the downbeat.

And Zinnie, pseudo-Hollywood, probably empty, certainly expensive, and not new, but a nice machine for all that.

Mildred certainly knew them. Mildred with the intense gray innocence of a vicious child, and the loneliness that made her seem vulnerable.

And Dr. Grantham, the good doctor with the bad case of lack of concept.

Lew Archer came to see them as monsters, with human faces. Perhaps one of them was the golden man for whom murder was done four times.

Ross Macdonald has once again grapple with some of the darkest forces in modern life. It was indeed of you ever had it. Macdonald's vivid picture of a world in which there are only good people and bad ones.

Dust jacket for A 13.1

A 13.2
First English edition, only printing (1958)

THE DOOMSTERS

by

JOHN ROSS MACDONALD

CASSELL & COMPANY LTD
LONDON

A 13.2: 4³/₄″ × 7¹/₄″

CASSELL & COMPANY LTD
35 Red Lion Square
London, W.C.1

and at

210 Queen Street, Melbourne; 26/30 Clarence Street, Sydney; 24 Wyndham Street, Auckland; 1068 Broadview Avenue, Toronto 6; P.O. Box 275, Cape Town; P.O. Box 11190, Johannesburg; Haroon Chambers, South Napier Road, Karachi; 13/14 Ajmeri Gate Extension, New Delhi 1; 15 Graham Road, Ballard Estate, Bombay 1; 17 Chittaranjan Avenue, Calcutta 13; P.O. Box 23, Colombo; Denmark House, (3rd floor), 84 Ampang Road, Kuala Lumpur; Avenida 9 de Julho 1138, São Paulo; Galeria Güemes, Escritorio 454/59 Florida 165, Buenos Aires; Marne 5b, Mexico 5, D.F.; Sanshin Building, 6 Kanda Mitos-chiro-cho, Chiyoda-ku, Tokyo; 25 rue Henri Barbusse, Paris 5e; 25 Ny Strandvej, Espergaerde, Copenhagen; Beulingstraat 2, Amsterdam-C; Bederstrasse 51, Zürich 2

© *1958 by John Ross Macdonald*
First published in Great Britain 1958

Set in 11 pt. Bembo type and
printed in Great Britain by Richard Clay and Company, Ltd.,
Bungay, Suffolk
F. 658

[i–vi] 1–225 [226]

Perfect binding. Signed: [A]⁸ B–I⁸ K–N⁸ O⁴ P⁸

Contents: p. i: half title; p. ii: blurb, 7 titles, fingerprint, 'A CRIME CONNOISSEUR | BOOK'; p. iii: title; p. iv: copyright; p. v: dedication; p. vi: disclaimer; pp. 1–225: text; p. 226: blank.

Typography and paper: 5³/₄″ (6″) × 3⁵/₈″. 38 lines per page. No running heads. Wove paper.

Binding: Brilliant green (#140) paper-covered boards with V-pattern (smooth). Spine stamped in black: '*THE | DOOMSTERS | [star] | John Ross | Macdonald | Crime | Connoisseur* | [rule] | *CASSELL*'. White endpapers. All edges trimmed. Also reported in orange and black bindings.

Dust Jacket: Front and spine black; back white. Front lettered in white with green, orange, and blue figures.

Publication: 3,674 copies of the first printing. Published 9 October 1958. 12/6.

THE DOOMSTERS
John Ross Macdonald

THE DOOMSTERS

John Ross Macdonald

A CASSELL CRIME CONNOISSEUR BOOK

A CRIME CONNOISSEUR BOOK

THRILLERS BY
JOHN ROSS MACDONALD

THE BARBAROUS COAST
"Tightly-plotted, tensely-written. Crowns Ross Macdonald king of the Chandler castle."—*Evening Standard*
"Unputdownable as usual."—*London Mystery Magazine*

FIND A VICTIM
"John Ross Macdonald is one of the most impressive American crime writers in the business today. He has often been favourably compared with Chandler to whom he owes a good deal. The difference is that while Macdonald is more sparing of the smart wisecrack he possesses an even more picturesque and imagistic style."—*Truth*

EXPERIENCE WITH EVIL
"He is just about the greatest discovery in years in the American thriller-writer field."—*Liverpool Post*

THE IVORY GRIN
"Mr. Macdonald must be ranked high among American thriller-writers. His evocations of scenes and people are as sharp as those of Mr Raymond Chandler."—*Times Literary Supplement*

THE WAY SOME PEOPLE DIE
"Can stand comparison with that master of all American thriller-writers and I can't think of higher praise."—*Daily Dispatch*

LONDON MYSTERY MAGAZINE:
"Every new book by Mr Macdonald proves that he is just about the best thriller-writer in America."

When Archer opened the door to the tall young man who was afraid of the light, he was letting the Doomsters in.

Who were the Doomsters? Carl certainly knew them—that was why Archer found him on the doorstep in a bad state of exhaustion and desperately in need of help. Zinnie knew them, though you wouldn't expect her to be haunted by memories—or conscience: Zinnie was pseudo-Hollywood, expensive and not very nice, but a nice machine for all that. Mildred certainly knew them and that was more understandable, with her grave innocence and the loneliness that made her seem vulnerable. And Dr. Grantland had his fill of them—he was a good doctor suffering from a bad case of lack of integrity. There was the red-headed woman, too, who drank time under the table; she knew them. But Archer didn't, until he got talked into helping Carl, and found himself always a lap behind the next murder.

It is two years since Macdonald produced his last thriller; the time has been well spent—this one is vintage stuff.

12'6 NET

Dust jacket for A 13.2

Printing: See copyright page.

Locations: BL (7 OCT 58); MJB (dj); UC-I (dj).

Proof copy: Bound in red paper wrappers with white label printed in black on front: 'THE DOOMSTERS | *by* | JOHN ROSS MACDONALD | *Publication date—9th October 1958* | *Published price—12/6 net* | CASSELL | PROOF ONLY'. *Location:* MJB.

A 13.3.a
Third edition: New York: Bantam, [1959].

#A2024. Wrappers. Reprinted 1967 and 1973.

A 13.3.b
Third edition, Canadian printing: Montreal: Bantam, 1959.

Wrappers. Not seen.

A 13.4
Fourth edition: London: Pan, [1960].

#G345. Wrappers. 36,239 copies. John Ross Macdonald.

A 13.5
Fifth edition: [London]: Fontana/Collins, [1971].

#2734. Wrappers. Five printings, 1971–1976.

A 13.6
Sixth edition: Archer in Jeopardy. New York: Knopf, 1979.

Includes *The Doomsters.* See AA 3.

Note: Condensed as "Bring the Killer to Justice," *Ellery Queen's Mystery Magazine* 39 (February 1962), 18–32, 62–80, 107–117. (The Bantam edition incorrectly states that *The Doomsters* was serialized in *EQMM* in 1958 as "Breakthrough.")

A 14 THE GALTON CASE

A 14.1.a
First edition, first printing (1959)

THE

GALTON CASE

Ross Macdonald

ALFRED A. KNOPF   *New York*   1959

A 14.1.a: 5³/₁₆″ × 7⁷/₁₆″

L. C. Catalog card number: 59-6222

© Ross Macdonald, 1959

THIS IS A BORZOI BOOK,
PUBLISHED BY ALFRED A. KNOPF, INC.

Copyright 1959 by Ross Macdonald. All rights reserved. No part of this book may be reproduced in any form without permission in writing from the publisher, except by a reviewer who may quote brief passages in a review to be printed in a magazine or newspaper. Manufactured in the United States of America. Published simultaneously in Canada by McClelland & Stewart Ltd.

FIRST EDITION

[i–x] [1–3] 4–242 [243–246]

$[1–8]^{16}$

Contents: pp. i–ii: blank; p. iii: blurb for *The Galton Case;* p. iv: card page, 9 titles; p. v: half title; p. vi: blank; p. vii: title; p. viii: copyright; p. ix: '*For John E. Smith, bookman*'; p. x: blank; p. 1: half title; p. 2: blank; pp. 3–242: text; pp. 243–244: blank; p. 245: note on author; p. 246: note on type.

Typography and paper: $5^{13}/16''$ (6") × $3^{5}/8''$. 35 lines per page. Running heads: versos only, 'THE GALTON CASE'. Wove paper.

Binding: Strong purplish red (#255) and light pink (#4) patterned paper-covered boards. Spine: '[in black on white panel] THE | *Galton* | *Case* | [rosette] | Ross | Macdonald | [on lower panel] ALFRED A. | KNOPF'. Back cover has black borzoi device on pale pink rectangle. Top and bottom edges trimmed. Top edge stained greenish blue.

Dust Jacket: Front and spine in shades of green; back white. Front lettered in white with pink and black art.

Publication: Published 16 March 1959. $3. Copyright #A 378594.

Printing: Composed, printed, and bound by H. Wolff, New York.

Locations: LC (MAR 2 1959); Lilly (dj); MJB (dj); UC-I (dj).

A 14.1.b
First edition, second printing: New York: Knopf, 1959.

Not seen.

Dust jacket for A 14.1.a

A 14.1.c
First edition, first English printing (1960)

THE
GALTON CASE

John Ross Macdonald

CASSELL · LONDON

A 14.1.c: $4^7/_8'' \times 7^1/_4''$

CASSELL & COMPANY LTD

35 Red Lion Square · London WC1

and at

MELBOURNE . SYDNEY · TORONTO · CAPE TOWN

JOHANNESBURG · AUCKLAND

© Ross Macdonald 1959

First published in Great Britain 1960

Printed in Great Britain by

Lowe & Brydone (Printers) Ltd., London, N.W.10

F.859

[i–viii] [1–3] 4–242 [243–244]

[A] B–I K–P⁸ Q⁶

Contents: pp. i–ii: blank; p. iii: blurb for *The Galton Case;* p. iv: 8 titles, fingerprint, 'A CRIME CONNOISSEUR BOOK'; p. v: title; p. vi: copyright; p. vii: dedication; p. viii: blank; p. 1: half title; p. 2: blank; pp. 3–242: text; pp. 243–244: blank.

Typography and paper: $5^{13}/_{16}''$ (6″) × $3^{5}/_{8}''$. 35 lines per page. Running heads: versos only, 'THE GALTON CASE'. Wove paper. Chapter headings altered.

Binding: Black paper-covered boards with V-pattern (smooth). Spine silverstamped: '*THE* | *GALTON* | *CASE* | [star] | *John* | *Ross* | *Macdonald* | [fingerprint] | *Crime* | *Connoisseur* | [rule] | *CASSELL'*. White endpapers. All edges trimmed.

Dust jacket: Front and spine illustrated in shades of brown; back white. Front lettered in black and white, with painting of desert scene. signed: M/M.

Publication: 4,817 copies of the first printing. Published 21 January 1960. 11/6.

Printing: See copyright page.

Locations: BL (12 JAN 60); MJB (dj).

A 14.2.a
Second edition, first printing: New York: Bantam, [1960].

#A2059. Wrappers. 16 printings, 1960–1983.

A 14.2.b
Second edition, Canadian printing: New York, Toronto, London: Bantam, [1980].

On copyright page: '15th printing . . . March 1980'.

#13235-0. Wrappers.

A 14.3
Third edition: London: Pan Books, [1962].

#G580. Wrappers. 51,058 copies. John Ross Macdonald.

Dust jacket for A 14.1.c

A 14.4
Fourth edition: London: Fontana/Collins, [1972].

2873. Wrappers.

A 14.5
Fifth edition: Archer at Large. New York: Knopf, 1970.

Includes *The Galton Case.* See AA 2.

A 14.6
Sixth edition: South Yarmouth, Mass.: John Curley, [1981].

Large-print edition. Wrappers.

A 15 THE FERGUSON AFFAIR

A 15.1.a
First edition, first printing (1960)

THE
FERGUSON
AFFAIR

Ross Macdonald

ALFRED · A · KNOPF   *New York*   1960

A 15.1.a: 5¹/₂″ × 8¹/₁₆″

> *Buenavista and Mountain Grove are imaginary cities; their citizens and denizens are all imaginary, intended to represent no actual persons living or dead. Some of them are fantastic.*
>
> R.M.

L. C. catalog card number: 60–9990

© Ross Macdonald, 1960

THIS IS A BORZOI BOOK,
PUBLISHED BY ALFRED A. KNOPF, INC.

Copyright 1960 by Ross Macdonald. All rights reserved. No part of this book may be reproduced in any form without permission in writing from the publisher, except by a reviewer who may quote brief passages in a review to be printed in a magazine or newspaper. Manufactured in the United States of America. Published simultaneously in Canada by McClelland & Stewart, Ltd.

FIRST EDITION

[i–iv] [1–3] 4–283 [284]

[1–9]^{16}

Contents: p. i: blurb on Ross Macdonald and blurb for *The Ferguson Affair;* p. ii: card page, 10 titles; p. iii: title; p. iv: copyright; p. 1: 'THE FERGUSON AFFAIR | *to Al Stump*'; p. 2: blank; pp. 3–283: text; p. 284: note on author and note on type.

Typography and paper: 5³/₄" (6") × 3³/₄". 32 lines per page. Running heads: versos only, 'THE FERGUSON AFFAIR'. Wove paper.

Binding: Three-piece binding. Light blue (#181) paper-covered boards and strong red (#12) V-cloth (smooth) shelfback. Front blindstamped: 'R [typographical flower] M'. Spine goldstamped: '[rules and type decorations] | THE | *Ferguson* | *Affair* | [rule] | Ross | Macdonald | [rules and type decorations] | *Knopf*'. Back has blindstamped rectangular borzoi device. White endpapers. Top and bottom edges trimmed. Top edge stained medium pink.

Dust jacket: Front black; spine yellow; back white. Front lettered in yellow, white, and gray with white, purple, and gray art. Signed: Muni.

Publication: Published 18 July 1960. $3.50. Copyright #A452812.

Printing: Composed, printed, and bound by H. Wolff, New York.

Locations: LC (JUL 5 1960); Lilly (dj); MJB (dj).

Dust jacket for A 15.1.a

A 15.1.b
First edition, second printing: New York: Knopf, 1960.

On copyright page: 'SECOND PRINTING, AUGUST 1960'.

A 15.1.c
First edition, third printing: New York: Knopf, 1960.

Not seen.

A 15.2.a
First English edition, first printing (1961)

THE
FERGUSON AFFAIR

by
ROSS MACDONALD

Published for
THE CRIME CLUB
by COLLINS 14 ST JAMES'S PLACE
LONDON

A 15.2.a: 4^{11}/$_{16}$″ × 7^{3}/$_{16}$″

> *Buenavista and Mountain Grove are imaginary cities;*
> *their citizens and denizens are all imaginary, intended*
> *to represent no actual persons living or dead. Some of*
> *them are fantastic.*
>
> R.M.
>
> © ROSS MACDONALD, 1960
> First published in Great Britain, 1961
> PRINTED IN GREAT BRITAIN
> COLLINS CLEAR-TYPE PRESS : LONDON AND GLASGOW

[1–6] 7–256

Perfect binding. Signed [A]^8 B–I^8 K–Q^8

Contents: p.1: half title; p. 2: blurb for *The Ferguson Affair* and 11 titles by Macdonald; p. 3: title; p. 4: copyright; p. 5: dedication; p. 6: blank; pp. 7–256: text.

Typography and paper: 5^3/$_4$″ (5^{15}/$_{16}$″) × 3^5/$_8$″. 38 lines per page. Running heads: rectos and versos, 'THE FERGUSON AFFAIR'. Wove paper.

Binding: Deep reddish orange (#36) paper-covered boards with V-pattern (smooth). Spine stamped in black: 'THE | FERGUSON | AFFAIR | ROSS | MACDONALD | [masked figure] | THE | CRIME | CLUB'. White endpapers. All edges trimmed.

Dust jacket: Front and spine greenish brown; back white. Front lettered in black and white with color art. Signed: Barbara Walton.

Publication: 6,958 copies of the first printing. Published 4 September 1961. 12/6.

Printing: See copyright page.

Locations: BL (12 SEP 61); Lilly (dj); MJB (dj); UC-I (dj).

A 15.2.b
Second edition, second printing: [London]: Collins/Fontana Books, [1963].

#859. Wrappers. 17,530 copies.

A 15.3
Third edition: The Ferguson Affair | Murder after a Fashion | Sing Me a Murder. Roslyn, N.Y.: Dectective Book Club, [1960].

A 15.4.a
Fourth edition, first printing: New York: Bantam, [1963].

#J2533. Wrappers. 5 printings, 1963–1970.

A 15.4.b
Fourth edition, Canadian printings: New York, Toronto, London: Bantam, [1967].

On copyright page: '3rd printing . . . October 1967'.

#F3518. Wrappers.

THE FERGUSON AFFAIR

Crime Club Choice

THE FERGUSON AFFAIR

Tess was also charged with selling stolen property was to be defended by Bill Gunnarson, a lawyer who had yet to make a name for himself. Bill believed her to be innocent, despite her screttiveness and her lies. Before the case came to trial a murder was committed — a murder obviously linked with the multiple burglaries which had led to the girl's arrest. The young lawyer found himself embarked on a tough, complicated and dangerous investigation; there were to be several more murders, and some bewildering developments, before Bill Gunnarson could get far ahead of the Ferguson Case. Very few readers will be ahead of Gunnarson in unravelling the story, or in penetrating the secrets of the character of the film star, Holly May, who was married to the oil magnate called Ferguson.

We are proud to publish this distinguished American crime novelist for the first time in the Crime Club. *The Ferguson Affair*, like Ross Macdonald's previous books, is a novel of quality. Real characters and true observations are worked into a plot that is complex, intriguing, and, finally, breathlessly exciting.

12s. 6d. n

Ross Macdonald

"Every new book by Mr. Macdonald proves that he is just about the best thriller-writer in America." *London Mystery Magazine*

"One of the most sharp and skilful of American crime novelists."
The Times Literary Supplement

"He is just about the greatest discovery in years in the American thriller-writer field." *Liverpool Post*

"A new star in the thriller firmament." *The Queen*

We shall publish as Crime Club choice for October, a novel by

RODERIC
JEFFRIES

Evidence of the Accused

of which Michael Gilbert has written:

"*I give him very high marks on two scores.*

First on his descriptions of police technique in the course of a murder investigation which are as full and as careful as anything I have read.

Secondly, on his adherence to a simple but most ingenious plot line."

Dust jacket for A 15.2.a

A 15.5

Fifth edition: New York, Toronto, London: Bantam, [1971].

#N6798. Wrappers. Six printings, 1971–1983.

Note: Condensed version syndicated by King Features, March–April 1963. Not seen.

A 16 THE WYCHERLY WOMAN

A 16.1
First edition, only printing (1961)

THE
WYCHERLY
WOMAN

Ross Macdonald

ALFRED · A · KNOPF   *New York*   1961

A 16.1: 5¹/₂″ × 8¹/₁₆″

> *The characters and incidents in this novel are all*
> *fictitious, and have no reference to any actual*
> *people or events.*
>
> L. C. catalog card number: 61-10295
>
> THIS IS A BORZOI BOOK,
> PUBLISHED BY ALFRED A. KNOPF, INC.
>
> *Copyright © 1961 by Ross Macdonald.*
> *All rights reserved. No part of this book may be repro-*
> *duced in any form without permission in writing from the*
> *publisher, except by a reviewer who may quote brief*
> *passages in a review to be printed in a magazine or news-*
> *paper. Manufactured in the United States of America.*
> *Published simultaneously in Canada by*
> *McClelland & Stewart, Ltd.*
>
> FIRST EDITION
>
> *A condensed version of this novel prepared by the author*
> *appeared in* Cosmopolitan *under the title of*
> Take My Daughter Home.

[i–viii] [1–3] 4–278 [279–280]

[1–9]^{16}

Contents: p. i: blank; p. ii: card page, 11 titles; p. iii: blurb for *The Wycherly Woman*; p. iv: blank; p. v: title; p. vi: copyright; p. vii: '*to Dorothy Olding*'; p. viii: blank; p. 1: half title; p. 2: blank; pp. 3–278: text; p. 279: note on author; p. 280: note on type.

Typography and paper: 6^{5}/16″ (6^{9}/16″) × 3^{13}/16″ 34 or 35 lines per page. Running heads: versos only, 'THE WYCHERLY WOMAN'. Wove paper.

Binding: Three-piece binding. Gray purplish red (#262) paper-covered boards and medium bluish green (#164) shelfback. Front blindstamped: 'R [typographical flower] M'. Spine goldstamped: '[rules and type decorations] | THE | *Wycherly* | *Woman* | [rule] | Ross | Macdonald | [rules and type decoration] | *Knopf*'. Back cover has blind-stamped borzoi device. White endpapers. Top and bottom edges trimmed. Top edge stained light yellow.

Dust jacket: Front and spine black; back white; front lettered in white and pink, with yellow and pink art. Signed: Muni.

Publication: Published 15 May 1961. $3.50. Copyright #A 499656.

Printing: Composed, printed, and bound by H. Wolff, New York.

Locations: LC (MAY 5 1961); Lilly (dj); MJB (dj); UC-I (dj).

Dust jacket for A 16.1

A 16.2 First English edition, only printing (*1962*)

THE WYCHERLY WOMAN

by
ROSS MACDONALD

Published for
THE CRIME CLUB
by COLLINS 14 ST JAMES'S PLACE
LONDON

A 16.2: 4³/₄″ × 7³/₁₆″

[1–6] 7–320

Perfect binding. Signed: [A]^8 B–I^8 K–U^8

Contents: p. 1: half title; p. 2: blurb for *The Wycherly Woman* and 10 titles by Macdonald; p. 3: title; p. 4: copyright; p. 5: dedication; p. 6: blank; pp. 7–320: text.

Typography and paper: 5³/₄″ (5¹⁵/₁₆″) × 3¹/₂″. 35 lines per page. Running heads: rectos and versos, 'THE WYCHERLY WOMAN'. Wove paper.

Binding: Deep reddish orange (#36) paper-covered boards with V-pattern (smooth). Spine stamped in black: 'THE | WYCHERLY | WOMAN | ROSS | MACDONALD | [masked figure] | THE | CRIME | CLUB'. White endpapers. All edges trimmed.

Dust jacket: Front and spine dark green; back white. Front lettered in red and yellow with color painting of woman.

Publication: 5,913 copies of the first printing. Published 19 April 1962. 15s.

Printing: See copyright page.

Locations: BL (13 APR 62); Lilly (dj); MJB (dj); UC-I (dj).

A 16.3
Third edition: New York, Toronto, London: Bantam, [1963].

#F2665. Wrappers. Reprinted 1968.

A 16.4
Fourth edition: [London]: Collins/Fontana Books, [1963].

#860. Wrappers. 39,669 copies. Reprinted 1965, 1971, 1973, 1979.

A 16.5
Fifth edition: New York, Toronto, London: Bantam, [1973].

#Q7267. Wrappers. Reprinted once.

Note: Condensed as "Take My Daughter Home," *Cosmopolitan* 150 (April 1961), 102–126.

Her name was
Phoebe Wycherly
Her age was
twenty-one

She was last seen alive at the San Francisco docks, three months before Lew Archer was hired to search for her. The search led him first to her family and her college friends, then far afield from the respectable and monied world where Phoebe had been brought up, into the criminal lower depths where life is valued lightly.

Ross Macdonald's new book has the texture of a good novel; the characters, ranging from an oil millionaire to an unemployed actress writing her 'true-confession' autobiography, are freshly seen; and, as always with Ross Macdonald, the narrative is fast-paced, leading up to an explosive climax.

15s. net

ROSS
MACDONALD

The
Wycherly
Woman

The Wycherly
Woman

ROSS
MACDONALD
joined the Crime Club with
THE FERGUSON
AFFAIR

"Ross Macdonald shows again his particular skill in the creation of character, very largely through crisp, credible dialogue; he is a dab-hand at constructing a tangled puzzle. Wry and funny in the Chandler manner." *Julian Symons, Sunday Times*

"An expert job, full of fizz." *Nicholas Blake, Sunday Telegraph*

ROSS
MACDONALD

'One of the most
sharp and skilful
of American
crime novelists'

THE TIMES LITERARY
SUPPLEMENT

'A new star in the
thriller firmament'

THE QUEEN

Dust jacket for A 16.2

A 17 THE ZEBRA-STRIPED HEARSE

A 17.1.a
First edition, first printing (1962)

THE
ZEBRA-
STRIPED
HEARSE

Ross Macdonald

ALFRED·A·KNOPF   *New York*   1962

A 17.1.a: 5^1/$_2$″ × 8^1/$_{16}$″

L. C. catalog card number: 62–18122

THIS IS A BORZOI BOOK,
PUBLISHED BY ALFRED A. KNOPF, INC.

Copyright © 1962 by Ross Macdonald. All rights reserved. No part of this book may be reproduced in any form without permission in writing from the publisher, except by a reviewer, who may quote brief passages in a review to be printed in a magazine or newspaper. Manufactured in the United States of America, and distributed by Random House, Inc. Published simultaneously in Toronto, Canada, by Random House of Canada, Limited.

FIRST EDITION

A condensed version of this novel prepared by the author appeared in *Cosmopolitan.*

[i–viii] [1–3] 4–278 [279–280]

[1–9]¹⁶

Contents: p. i: blank; p. ii: card page, 12 titles; p. iii: blurb for *The Zebra-Striped Hearse;* p. iv: blank; p. v: title; p. vi: copyright; p. vii: '*To Harris W. Seed*'; p. viii: disclaimer; p. 1: half title; p. 2: blank; pp. 3–278: text; p. 279: note on author; p. 280: note on type.

Typography and paper: 6⁵/₁₆″ (6⁹/₁₆″) × 3⁷/₈″. 35 lines per page. Running heads: versos only, 'THE ZEBRA-STRIPED HEARSE'. Wove paper.

Binding: Three-piece binding: Medium yellow (#87) paper-covered boards and black V-cloth (smooth) shelfback. Front blindstamped: 'R [typographical flower] M'. Spine goldstamped: '[rule and type decorations] | THE | *Zebra-* | *Striped* | *Hearse* | [rule] | Ross | Macdonald | [rules and type decorations] | *Knopf*'. Blindstamped borzoi device on back. White endpapers. Top and bottom edges trimmed. Top edge stained deep yellowish pink.

Dust jacket: Front, spine, and back white; front lettered in pink, black, and gray with yellow, black-and-white, gray, and tan art.

Publication: Published 5 November 1962. $3.50. Copyright #A 599282.

the zebra-striped hearse

HARRIET was a big girl, twenty-five on her next birthday, but her father, Colonel Blackwell, persisted in treating her as a little one. When she came back from Mexico with a man she planned to marry, the Colonel assumed this match could not be suitable. Burke Damis, the prospective bridegroom, claimed to be a serious painter. Harriet considered him a genius, but nobody else had ever heard of him. So the Colonel hired Archer to look into Damis's background. Almost at once he discovered the body of a man stabbed to death with an icepick. Meanwhile Damis and Harriet had dropped out of sight.

The story moves with grace and speed and steadily mounting excitement across the map of California and through its society, from Los Angeles to the Bay area, from the American-Mexican border at Tijuana and Chapala to the floating population of gay young people and the girls on the south shore of Lake Tahoe.

This is Mr. Macdonald's tenth book about the physical and moral adventures of Lew Archer, and perhaps the most fascinating of a brilliantly sustained, and widely acclaimed, series. Like Raymond Chandler and Dashiell Hammett before him, Ross Macdonald writes for the general literate public. That mystery fans also like his work is all to the good.

the zebra-striped hearse

a new, powerful and fast-paced novel by the author of
THE WYCHERLY WOMAN and THE FERGUSON AFFAIR

ROSS MACDONALD

the zebra-striped hearse | ROSS MACDONALD

ALFRED A. KNOPF

What the reviewers said about
Ross Macdonald's last two books

THE WYCHERLY WOMAN

"Mr. Macdonald's prose is crisp, pungent and exemplary and so are his sensibilities. First-rate." —*New York Herald Tribune*

"This is not only a powerful suspense story, it is an exciting novel, brilliantly planned and skillfully written." —*St. Louis Post-Dispatch*

"You not only can read [Macdonald's mysteries] a second time, you should; that's when you'll truly notice all the intricate ironies, paradoxes, and poetic leitmotifs of which they are built." —*The New York Post*

"Ross Macdonald is one of the best living writers of the whipcord thriller, with not one spare ounce of flesh on the crackling dialogue. It's the kind of style and story that has a Bogart twist to its mouth." —*The Bookman*

THE FERGUSON AFFAIR

"A marvel of plotting. . . . A disturbing novel of human beings and their tormented and tormenting relationships." —*Anthony Boucher, The New York Times*

"Macdonald's characterizations are skillful, his writing style is literate, and his plot . . . is varied and exciting. The result is a winner." —*New Orleans Times-Picayune*

"Provocative characterizations and polished writing make it top-drawer suspense fare." —*Des Moines Register*

Alfred A. Knopf, Publisher   NEW YORK

PHOTO: HAL BOUCHER

Ross Macdonald
was born near San Francisco in 1915. He was educated in Canadian schools, traveled widely in Europe, and acquired advanced degrees and a Phi Beta Kappa key at the University of Michigan. In 1938 he married a Canadian girl who is now well known as the novelist Margaret Millar. Mr. Macdonald (Kenneth Millar in private life) taught school and college, and served as Communication Officer aboard an escort carrier in the Pacific. For the past sixteen years he has lived in Santa Barbara and written mystery novels about the explosively changing society of his native state. His hobbies include sailing, tower diving, all-year swimming, and literary criticism.

Dust jacket for A 17.1.a

Printing: Composed, printed, and bound by H. Wolff, New York.

Locations: LC (NOV 5 1962); Lilly (dj); MJB (dj); UC-I (dj).

A 17.1.b
First edition, second printing: New York: Knopf, 1962.

On copyright page: 'SECOND PRINTING, DECEMBER 1962'.

A 17.1.c
First edition, third printing: New York: Knopf [1963].

Mystery Guild.

A 17.2.a
First English edition, first printing (1963)

THE
ZEBRA-STRIPED
HEARSE

by
ROSS MACDONALD

Published for

THE CRIME CLUB

by COLLINS 14 ST JAMES'S PLACE
LONDON

A 17.2.a: 4^{11}/$_{16}$″ × 7^{3}/$_{16}$″

First Published in Great Britain 1963

The people in this novel are fortunately all imaginary, and were invented without reference to any actual people living or dead.

R.M.

© ROSS MACDONALD, 1962

PRINTED IN GREAT BRITAIN

COLLINS CLEAR-TYPE PRESS : LONDON AND GLASGOW

[1–6] 7–256

Perfect binding. Signed: [A]^8 B–I^8 K–Q^8

Contents: p. 1: half title; p. 2: blurb for *The Zebra-Striped Hearse* and 13 titles by Macdonald; p. 3: title; p. 4: copyright; p. 5: dedication; p. 6: blank; pp. 7–256: text.

Typography and paper: 5^5/$_8$″ (5^7/$_8$″) × 3^{11}/$_{16}$″. 39 lines per page. Running heads: rectos and versos, 'THE ZEBRA-STRIPED HEARSE'. Wove paper.

Binding: Deep reddish orange (#36) paper-covered boards with V-pattern (smooth). Spine: '[black] THE | ZEBRA- | STRIPED | HEARSE | Ross | MACDONALD | [masked figure] | THE | CRIME | CLUB'. White endpapers. All edges trimmed.

Dust jacket: Front and spine in red and black; back white. Front lettered in white with color portrait of woman. Signed: Barbara Walton.

Publication: 6,473 copies of the first printing. Published 8 July 1963. 15s.

Printing: See copyright page.

Locations: BL (27 JUN 63); MJB (dj); UC-I (dj).

A 17.2.b
Second edition, second printing: [London]: Collins/Fontana Books, [1965].

#1093. Wrappers. Reprinted 1971, 1978.

A 17.3
Third edition: New York: Bantam, [1964].

#F2715. Wrappers. 11 printings, 1964–1978. Canadian printing not seen.

A 17.4
Fourth edition: Barbouze | The Zebra-Striped Hearse | The Cincinnati Kid. London: Odhams, [1964].

Man's Book.

A 17.5
Fifth edition: Archer in Jeopardy. New York: Knopf, 1979.

Includes *The Zebra-Striped Hearse.* See AA 3.

Dust jacket for A 17.2.a

ROSS
macdonald

the
zebra-
striped
hearse

ROSS macdonald
the zebra-striped hearse

crime club

THE AUTHOR

Ross Macdonald was born in California of Canadian-American ancestry. He was educated in Canada, and married a Canadian girl who is now a well known novelist writing under the name Margaret Millar. After several years of high-school teaching, he was given a fellowship at the University of Michigan, and took his doctorate with a study of Coleridge's psychology. He joined the U.S. Navy in 1944, and served as a communications officer on an escort carrier. He is a National Director of the Mystery Writers of America.

'Every

new book by

Mr. Macdonald

proves that

he is just about

the best

thriller-writer

in America'

LONDON
MYSTERY
MAGAZINE

LEW ARCHER was hired by the bride's father to stop a wedding; he was to investigate the mysterious and romantic-looking young painter with whom Harriet was infatuated, and show him up as a good-for-nothing. Colonel Blackwell was very proprietary about his daughter although she was twenty-four years old.

Enquiring into the young man's past, Archer soon finds not mere dissipation or minor delinquency—but murder. As his investigation proceeds, this first murder leads to others. The story moves with speed and steadily mounting excitement across the map of California and through its society, from Los Angeles to the floating population of gamblers and their girls at Lake Tahoe.

This is the tenth in this series of celebrated crime novels by Ross Macdonald. Brilliantly written and placed, its climax comes as a triple shock and an all-too-credible revelation.

15s. net

A 17.6

Sixth edition: South Yarmouth, Mass.: John Curley, [1980].

Large-print edition. Wrappers.

Note: Condensed in *Cosmopolitan* 153 (September 1962), 102, 104–106, 108–129.

A 18 THE CHILL

A 18.1.a
First edition, first printing (1964)

THE
CHILL

Ross Macdonald

ALFRED·A·KNOPF   *New York*   1964

A 18.1.a: 5^1/$_2$″ × 8^1/$_{16}$″

L. C. catalog card number: 63–20837

THIS IS A BORZOI BOOK,
PUBLISHED IN NEW YORK BY ALFRED A. KNOPF, INC.

Copyright © 1963 by Ross MACDONALD. All rights reserved. No part of this book may be reproduced in any form without permission in writing from the publisher, except by a reviewer, who may quote brief passages in a review to be printed in a magazine or newspaper. Manufactured in the United States of America, and distributed by Random House, Inc. Published simultaneously in Toronto, Canada, by Random House of Canada, Limited.

F I R S T   E D I T I O N

A condensed version of this novel prepared by the author appeared in *Cosmopolitan.*

The lines from the poem "Among School Children" quoted in Chapter 29 are reprinted from *The Collected Poems of W. B. Yeats* by permission of The Macmillan Company.

[i–viii] [1–3] 4–279 [280]

[1–9]¹⁶

Contents: p. i: blank; p. ii: card page, 13 titles; p. iii: blurb for *The Chill;* p. iv: blank; p. v: title; p. vi: copyright; p. vii: *'To R. W. Lid';* p. viii: disclaimer; p. 1: half title; p. 2: blank; pp. 3–279: text; p. 280: note on type.

Typography and paper: 6¹⁄₄″ (6¹⁄₂″) × 3¹³⁄₁₆″. 34 lines per page. Running heads: versos only, 'THE CHILL'. Wove paper.

Binding: Three-piece binding: Light blue (#181) paper-covered boards and deep red (#13) V-cloth (smooth) shelfback. Front blindstamped: 'R [typographical flower] M'. Spine goldstamped: '[rules and type decorations] | THE | *Chill* | [rule] | Ross | Macdonald | [rules and type decorations | *Knopf*'. Back: blindstamped borzoi device. White endpapers. Top and bottom edges trimmed. Top edge stained medium purplish red.

Dust jacket: Front white; spine purple; back white. Front lettered in purple and blue.

Publication: Published 13 January 1964. $3.95. Copyright #A671470.

The Chill

marks the eleventh appearance of Ross Macdonald's California detective, Lew Archer. Hired to trace a runaway bride, Archer uncovers a trail of murder that leads halfway across America and twenty years into the past. Beyond that, it need only be said that the story is every bit as exciting, baffling, and ultimately satisfying as would be expected from the author of *The Zebra-Striped Hearse*.

In the direct line of succession that reaches from Dashiell Hammett to Raymond Chandler, Ross Macdonald adds, to the crackling dialogue and narrative tightness of his illustrious predecessors, impressive qualities of his own: a depth of psychological understanding, a sureness in handling a wide variety of social milieux, and a dazzling, unpredictable plot.

All this explains why Mr. Macdonald's novels "even appeal to people who don't ordinarily read mysteries," as *Publishers Weekly* says, and why they are gaining an increasing audience among lovers of good fiction.

ROSS MACDONALD

THE Chill

ROSS MACDONALD

a new novel by the author of
THE ZEBRA-STRIPED HEARSE

ALFRED A. KNOPF

ROSS MACDONALD

is one of the best living writers of the whipped thriller, with not one spare ounce of flesh on the crackling dialogue. It's the kind of style and story that has a Bogart twist to its mouth.
—*The Bookman*

THE ZEBRA-STRIPED HEARSE (1962)

This is Mr. Macdonald's twelfth performance in the manner that Dashiell Hammett invented, that Raymond Chandler elaborated, and that he himself has refined, and it is a model of his excellence. That is to say, it has character, statement, and style."
—*The New Yorker*

"Macdonald has gradually created his own form ... by turning to the lives of quiet bourgeois desperation that are the legacy of California's passionate belief in unreality.... The plot is extremely complicated but it is also the perfect instrument for rendering, question by question, the way point-fours in Malibu leads to colonies in Mexico, Nevada, and other celebration of the grotesque, and how these, in turn, lead to horror and violence. It is a limited and stylized mode, but it dramatizes, as few others can, genuinely contemporary experience."
—Roxan Saiz in *Hudson Review*

Alfred A. Knopf, Publisher, New York

Ross Macdonald

was born near San Francisco in 1915. He was educated in Canadian schools, traveled widely in Europe, and acquired advanced degrees and a Phi Beta Kappa key at the University of Michigan. In 1938 he married a Canadian girl who is now well known as the novelist Margaret Millar. Mr. Macdonald (Kenneth Millar in private life) taught school and later college, and served in Communications Office aboard an escort carrier in the Pacific. For the past seventeen years he has lived in Santa Barbara and written mystery novels about the explosively changing society of his native state. His hobbies include sailing, bird watching, all-year swimming, and literary criticism.

Dust Jacket for A 18.1.a

Printing: Manufactured by Doubleday & Co., Hanover, Pa., and Haddon Craftsmen, Scranton, Pa.

Locations: LC (JAN 7 1964); Lilly (dj); MJB (dj); UC-I (dj).

A 18.1.b
First edition, second printing: New York: Knopf, [1964].

Mystery Guild.

A 18.2.a
First English edition, first printing (1964)

THE CHILL

by
ROSS MACDONALD

Published for

THE CRIME CLUB

by COLLINS, 14 ST JAMES'S PLACE
LONDON

A 18.2.a: $4^{11}/_{16}'' \times 7^3/_{16}''$

© ROSS MACDONALD, 1963
FIRST PUBLISHED IN GREAT BRITAIN 1964
PRINTED IN GREAT BRITAIN
COLLINS CLEAR-TYPE PRESS: LONDON AND GLASGOW

[1–8] 9–256

Perfect binding. Signed: [A]⁸ B–I⁸ K–Q⁸

Contents: p. 1: half title; p. 2: blurb for *The Chill* and 12 titles by Macdonald; p. 3: title; p. 4: copyright; p.5: dedication; p. 6: disclaimer; p. 7: acknowledgments; p. 8: blank; pp. 9–256: text.

Typography and paper: $5^{3}/_{4}''$ ($5^{15}/_{16}''$) × $3^{11}/_{16}''$. 40 lines per page. Running heads: rectos and versos, 'THE CHILL'. Wove paper.

Binding: Dark blue (#183) and deep reddish orange (#36) paper-covered boards with B-pattern (linen) front and back divided by dark blue vertical rule from shelfback of deep reddish orange paper with V-pattern (smooth). Spine goldstamped: 'THE | CHILL | ROSS | MACDONALD | [masked figure] | THE | CRIME | CLUB'. White endpapers. All edges trimmed.

Dust jacket: Front and spine pink and blue; back white. Front lettered in white and black.

Publication: 6,876 copies of the first printing. Published 9 November 1964. 15s.

Printing: See copyright page.

Locations: BL (27 OCT 64); Lilly (dj); MJB (dj); UC-I (dj).

A 18.2.b
Second edition, second printing: [London]: Collins/Fontana Books, [1966].

#1343. 21,550 copies. Wrappers. 4 printings, 1966–1979.

A 18.3.a
Third edition: New York, Toronto, London: Bantam, [1965].

#F2913. Wrappers. 14 printings, 1965–1983.

A 18.3.b
Third edition, Canadian printing: New York, Toronto, London: Bantam, [1965].

On copyright page: 'Bantam edition published March 1965'.

#F2913. Wrappers.

A 18.4
Fourth edition: Archer at Large. New York: Knopf, 1970.

Includes *The Chill.* See AA 2.

Note: Condensed in *Cosmopolitan* 155 (August 1963), 106, 108–129. Also syndicated by King Features, April–May 1964. Not seen.

Hired to trace a runaway bride, Lew Archer uncovers a trail of murder that leads halfway across America and twenty years into the past. Beyond that, it need only be said that the story is every bit as exciting, baffling, and ultimately satisfying as would be expected from the author of *The Zebra-Striped Hearse*.

In the direct line of succession that reaches from Dashiell Hammett to Raymond Chandler, Ross Macdonald adds, to the crackling dialogue and narrative tightness of his illustrious predecessors, impressive qualities of his own: a depth of psychological understanding, a sureness in handling a wide variety of social milieus, and a dazzling, unpredictable plot.

The Zebra-Striped Hearse by Ross Macdonald. Don't miss this brilliant Californian private-eye thriller, in the school of Raymond Chandler and worthy of the master.' Queen

15s. net

CRIME CLUB CHOICE

ROSS MACDONALD

THE Chill

ROSS MACDONALD the Chill

CRIME CLUB CHOICE

COLLINS

A new novel with Lew Archer 'Brilliant private eye, worthy of Raymond Chandler' Queen

Also by
ROSS MACDONALD
'One of the most sharp and skilful of American crime novelists.'
The Times Literary Supplement

The Wycherley Woman
'Ross Macdonald is one of the best living writers of the whodunnit thriller, with not one surplus ounce of flesh on the crackling dialogue. This is an excellent thriller, fast-moving and sharp-eyed, spare as a brush-drawing, masculine as the smell of a tweed jacket. But don't try to tell me that it isn't a woman's book as well.'
Susan Cooper, Bookman

'A highly accomplished and individual piece of work.'
Julian Symons, Sunday Times

The Ferguson Affair
'An expert job, full of fizz.'
Nicholas Blake, Sunday Telegraph

'Ross Macdonald shows again his particular skill in the creation of character; very largely through crisp, credible dialogue; he is a dab-hand at constructing a tangled puzzle. Wry and funny in the Chandler manner.'
Julian Symons, Sunday Times

The
Zebra-Striped
Hearse

ROSS
MACDONALD

'Rich stilton.
This is
the finest yet
of Macdonald's
Crime Studies.'

PETER PHILLIPS,
DAILY HERALD

Dust jacket for A 18.2.a

A 19 THE FAR SIDE OF THE DOLLAR

A 19.1.a
First edition, first printing (1965)

THE
FAR SIDE
OF
THE DOLLAR

Ross Macdonald

NEW YORK : ALFRED · A · KNOPF : 1965

A 19.1.a: $5^{9}/_{16}$″ × $8^{1}/_{16}$″

L. C. catalog card number: 65-10103

THIS IS A BORZOI BOOK,
PUBLISHED BY ALFRED A. KNOPF, INC.

Copyright © 1964 by Ross MACDONALD. All rights reserved. No part of this book may be reproduced in any form without permission in writing from the publisher, except by a reviewer, who may quote brief passages in a review to be printed in a magazine or newspaper. Manufactured in the United States of America, and distributed by Random House, Inc. Published simultaneously in Toronto, Canada, by Random House of Canada, Limited.

FIRST EDITION

A condensed version of this novel appeared in *Cosmopolitan* under the title *The Far Side.*

[i–viii] [1–3] 4–247 [248]

[1–8]^{16}

Contents: p. i: blank; p. ii: card page, 14 titles; p. iii: blurb for *The Far Side of the Dollar;* p. iv: blank; p. v: title; p. vi: copyright; p. vii: *'TO ALFRED';* p. viii: disclaimer; p. 1: half title; p. 2: blank; pp. 3–247: text; p. 248: note on type.

Typography and paper: 6¼″ (6½″) × 3¹⁵/₁₆″. 38 lines per page. Running heads: versos only, 'THE FAR SIDE OF THE DOLLAR'. Wove paper.

Binding: Three-piece binding: brownish gray (#64) paper-covered boards and strong green (#141) shelfback. Front blindstamped: 'R [typographical flower] M'. Spine gold-stamped: '[rules and type decorations] | THE | *Far Side* | OF THE | *Dollar* | [rule] | Ross | Macdonald | [rules and type decorations] | *Knopf'*. Back: blindstamped borzoi device. White endpapers. Top and bottom edges trimmed. Top edge stained yellow.

Dust jacket: Front black; spine blue; back white. Front lettered in blue, white, and yellowish-green with art in black and gray.

Publication: Published 18 January 1965. $3.95. Copyright #A 734788.

Printing: Composed, printed, and bound by Haddon Craftsmen, Scranton, Pa.

Locations: LC (DEC 29 1964); Lilly (dj); MJB (dj); UC-I (dj).

A 19.1.b
First edition, second printing: New York: Knopf, 1965.

Mystery Guild.

THE *Far Side*
OF THE *Dollar*

To the hard-boiled story of violence and death, Ross Macdonald has brought substance and depth of characterization. It is often said that he follows in the tradition of Dashiell Hammett and Raymond Chandler, but Macdonald has actually broken new ground. His novels have a social range and moral dimension that, in combination with a striking prose style and narrative drive, provide the reader with a rewarding experience.

In this new and moving novel, Lew Archer, Macdonald's celebrated California investigator, is hired by the principal of a private reform school, to trace a missing boy. What appears to be an ordinary matter of juvenile delinquency is suddenly magnified, as Archer plunges into a web of murder and extortion. He ranges all over the Far West, tracking down men and women who are pursuing the fast buck, and hating to be reminded of what is waiting on the far side of the last dollar.

JACKET DESIGN BY ARTHUR HAWKINS

ROSS MACDONALD

THE CHILL
THE ZEBRA-STRIPED HEARSE

THE
FAR
SIDE
OF
THE
DOLLAR

an exciting new novel!

ROSS
MACDONALD

THE
FAR
SIDE
OF
THE
DOLLAR

THE CHILL   (1964)

"The finest of Mr. Macdonald's prestige works."
Dorothy B. Hughes, *New York Herald Tribune*

"Macdonald should not be limited in audience to connoisseurs of mystery fiction. He is one of a handful of writers in the genre whose worth and quality surpass the limitations of the form."
Robert Kirsch, *Los Angeles Times*

"Ross Macdonald in recent years has become the best writer we have about California and one of the country's best novelists."
Roger Sale, *Argus*

THE ZEBRA-STRIPED HEARSE   (1962)

"This is Mr. Macdonald's twelfth performance in the manner that Dashiell Hammett invented, that Raymond Chandler elaborated, and that he himself has refined, and it is a model of his excellence. That is to say, it has character, statement, and style."
The New Yorker

"Stands solidly as a first rate novel. Ross Macdonald gives to the detective story that accent of class that the late Raymond Chandler did ... What makes this book a standout is the taut writing, the excellent delineation of character, and the interesting plot."
Sergeant Kinman, *Chicago Tribune*

Alfred·A·Knopf, Publisher, New York

PHOTO: HAL MOORE

Ross Macdonald

was born, near San Francisco in 1915. He was educated in Canadian schools, traveled widely in Europe, and acquired advanced degrees and a Phi Beta Kappa key at the University of Michigan. In 1938 he married a Canadian girl who is now well known as the novelist Margaret Millar. Mr. Macdonald (Kenneth Millar) in private life: taught school and later college, and served as Communications Officer aboard an escort carrier in the Pacific. For the past seventeen years he has lived in Santa Barbara and written many novels about the explosively changing society of his native state. His hobbies include sailing, bird watching, all-year swimming, and literary criticism.

PRINTED IN U.S.A.

Dust jacket for A 19.1.a

A 19.2.a
First English edition, first printing (1965)

THE FAR SIDE
OF THE DOLLAR

by
ROSS MACDONALD

Published for

THE CRIME CLUB

by COLLINS, 14 ST JAMES'S PLACE
LONDON

A 19.2.a: 4³/₄″ × 7³/₁₆

First published in Great Britain 1965

© ROSS MACDONALD, 1964

PRINTED IN GREAT BRITAIN

COLLINS CLEAR-TYPE PRESS : LONDON AND GLASGOW

[1–6] 7–256

Perfect binding. Signed: [A]^8 B–I^8 L–Q^8

Contents: p. 1: half title; p. 2: blurb, 13 titles; p. 3: title; p. 4: copyright; p. 5: dedication; p. 6: disclaimer; pp. 7–256: text.

Typography and paper: 5³/₄″ (5¹⁵/₁₆″) × 3⁵/₈″. 38 lines per page. Running heads: rectos and versos, 'THE FAR SIDE OF THE DOLLAR'. Wove paper.

Binding: Dark blue (#183) and deep reddish orange (#36) paper-covered boards with B-pattern (linen) divided by vertical dark blue rule from deep reddish orange paper shelfback with V-pattern (smooth). Spine goldstamped: 'THE | FAR SIDE | OF THE | DOLLAR | ROSS | MACDONALD | [masked figure] | THE | CRIME | CLUB'. White endpapers. All edges trimmed.

Dust jacket: Front and spine orange, back white. Front lettered in black and white with gray art.

Publication: 6,574 copies of the first printing. Published 6 September 1965. 16s.

Printing: See copyright page.

Locations: BL (31 AUG 65); MJB (dj); UC-I (dj).

A 19.2.b
Second edition, second printing: [London]: Collins/Fontana Books, [1967].

#1546. Wrappers. 17,494 copies.

A 19.3
Third edition: New York, Toronto, London: Bantam, [1966].

#F3159. Wrappers. 7 printings.

A 19.4
Fourth edition: Great Stories of Suspense, ed. Ross Macdonald. New York: Knopf, 1974.

Includes *The Far Side of the Dollar,* pp. 607–805. See A 26.

A 19.5
Fifth edition: South Yarmouth, Mass.: John Curley, [1980].

Large-print edition. Wrappers.

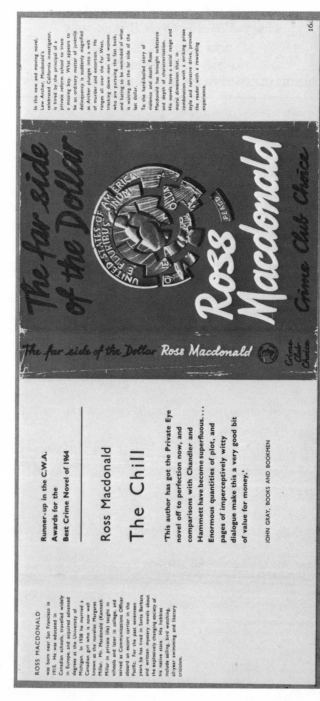

Dust jacket for A 19.2.a

A 19.6

Sixth edition: Columbia, S.C. & Bloomfield Hills, Mich.: Bruccoli Clark, 1982.

"Manuscript Edition." 221 numbered copies, each with a leaf of the revised typescript. Includes previously unpublished chapter. The edition was withdrawn from sale after review copies (without the inserted typescript leaf) were distributed.

Note: Condensed as "The Far Side," *Cosmopolitan* 157 (September 1964), 100, 102–109, 111–117, 121–130.

A 20 BLACK MONEY

A 20.1.a
First edition, first printing (1966)

BLACK MONEY

Ross Macdonald

ALFRED·A·KNOPF   *New York*   1966

A 20.1.a: 5⁹/₁₆″ × 8¹/₁₆″

L. C. catalog card number: 66–10031

THIS IS A BORZOI BOOK,
PUBLISHED BY ALFRED A. KNOPF, INC.

FIRST EDITION

A condensed version of this novel appeared in *Cosmopolitan* under the title *The Demon Lover*.

[i–x] [1–3] 4–238 [239–246]

[1–8]^{16}

Contents: pp. i–iii: blank; p. iv: card page, 15 titles; p. v: blurb for *Black Money;* p. vi: blank; p. vii: title; p. viii: copyright; p. ix: 'To Robert Easton'; p. x: disclaimer; p. 1: half title; p. 2: blank; pp. 3–238: text; p. 239: blank; p. 240: note on type; p. 241: note on author; pp. 242–246: blank.

Typography and paper: 6⅜″ (6⁹/₁₆″) × 3¹³/₁₆″. 37 or 38 lines per page. Running heads: rectos only, 'BLACK MONEY'. Wove paper.

Binding: Three-piece binding: Brilliant blue (#177) paper-covered boards with dark reddish brown (#44) V-cloth (smooth) shelfback. Front blindstamped: 'R [typographical flower] M'. Spine goldstamped: '[rules and type decorations] *Black* | *Money* | [rule] | Ross | Macdonald | [rules and type decorations] | *Knopf*'. Back: blindstamped borzoi device. White endpapers. Top and bottom edges trimmed. Top edge stained light blue.

Dust jacket: Front and spine black; back white with red panel at top and pink panel at bottom. Front lettered in pink with gray, black, white and red art.

Publication: Published 10 January 1966. $3.95. Copyright #A 809439.

Printing: Composed, printed, and bound by Haddon Craftsmen, Scranton, Pa.

Locations: Lilly (dj); MJB (dj); UC-I (dj).

Ross Macdonald's famous private detective, Lew Archer, is the kind of man you can drop a secret into and never hear it hit bottom. In his thirteenth and strangest case he explores the secret life of a rich California residential community. A beautiful young woman has jilted her fiancé and taken up with a mysterious character who represents himself as a French political refugee. Hired to investigate this man, Archer becomes involved in several murders and a gigantic swindle. Running through the case, as a central theme in this morally disturbing novel, is the corrupting influence of the underworld and its money in our society.

Black Money is the most individual of the brilliant series of novels that have won Ross Macdonald international recognition.

Jacket design by Adelson & Eichinger

1/66

THE FAR SIDE OF THE DOLLAR (1965)

"Without in the least slating my admiration for Dashiell Hammett and Raymond Chandler, I should like to venture the heretical suggestion that Ross Macdonald is a better novelist than either of them."

ANTHONY BOUCHER, *The New York Times Book Review*

"Ross Macdonald is an important American novelist."

WILLIAM HOGAN, *San Francisco Chronicle*

THE CHILL (1964)

"The finest of Mr. Macdonald's prestige works."

DOROTHY B. HUGHES, *New York Herald Tribune*

"Macdonald should not be limited in audience to connoisseurs of mystery fiction. He is one of a handful of writers in the genre whose worth and quality surpass the limitations of the form."

ROBERT KIRSCH, *Los Angeles Times*

"Ross Macdonald in recent years has become the best writer we have about California and one of the country's best novelists."

ROGER SALE, *Argus*

Ross Macdonald was born near San Francisco in 1915. He was educated in Canadian schools, traveled widely in Europe, and acquired advanced degrees and a Phi Beta Kappa key at the University of Michigan. In 1938 he married a Canadian girl who is now well known as the novelist Margaret Millar. Mr. Macdonald (Kenneth Millar in private life) taught school and later college, and served as Communications Officer aboard an escort carrier in the Pacific. For the past twenty years he has lived in Santa Barbara and has written mystery novels about the explosively changing society of his native state. His main interests, outside of literature, are conservation and politics. He is the current president of Mystery Writers of America. In 1964 his novel *The Chill* was given a Silver Dagger award by the Crime Writers' Association of Great Britain.

PHOTO: ALFRED A. LOWRY

BLACK MONEY
Ross Macdonald

BLACK MONEY
Ross Macdonald

ALFRED A KNOPF

Alfred A Knopf, Publisher, New York

PRINTED IN U.S.A.

Dust jacket for A 20.1.a

A 20.1.b
First edition, second printing: New York: Knopf, 1966.

Mystery Guild.

A 20.2.a
First English edition, first printing (1966)

BLACK MONEY

by
ROSS MACDONALD

Published for
THE CRIME CLUB
by COLLINS 14 ST JAMES'S PLACE
LONDON

A 20.2.a: 4³/₄″ × 7³/₁₆″

© 1965, 1966 BY ROSS MACDONALD
FIRST PUBLISHED IN GREAT BRITAIN 1966
PRINTED IN GREAT BRITAIN
COLLINS CLEAR-TYPE PRESS : LONDON AND GLASGOW

[1–6] 7–255 [256]

Perfect binding. Signed: [A]⁸ B–I⁸ K–Q⁸

Contents: p. 1: half title; p. 2: blurb for *Black Money* and 14 titles by Macdonald; p. 3: title; p. 4: copyright; p. 5: dedication; p. 6: disclaimer; pp. 7–255: text; p. 256: blank.

Typography and paper: $5^{11}/_{16}''$ ($5^7/_8''$) × $3^{11}/_{16}''$. 36 lines per page. Wove paper. Running heads: rectos and versos, 'BLACK MONEY'.

Binding: Deep reddish orange (#36) paper-covered boards with light brown B-pattern (linen). Spine goldstamped: 'BLACK | MONEY | ROSS | MACDONALD | [masked figure] | THE | CRIME | CLUB'. White endpapers. All edges trimmed.

Publication: 6,420 copies of the first printing. Published 8 August 1966. 16s.

Dust jacket: Front and spine in turquoise; back white. Front lettered in white with black and red art. Silver wraparound band printed in black announcing awards won by *The Far Side of The Dollar* and *The Chill.*

Printing: See copyright page.

Locations: BL (22 JUL 66); Lilly (dj); MJB (dj); UC-I (dj).

Note: English book club edition reported but not seen. 31,252 copies.

A 20.2.b
Second edition, second printing: [London]: Collins/Fontana, [1968].

Wrappers. 18,912 copies. Reprinted 1970.

A 20.3
Third edition: New York, Toronto, London: Bantam, [1967].

#F3320. Wrappers. Reprinted 1973.

A 20.4
Fourth edition: The Wrecking of Offshore Five | Trial by Battle | Black Money. London: Odhams, [1968].

Man's Book.

A 20.5
Fifth edition: Archer at Large. New York: Knopf, 1970.

Includes *Black Money.* See AA 2.

Note: Condensed as "The Demon Lover," *Cosmopolitan* 159 (December 1965), 110–118, 120–133, 136–139.

Runner up in the
C.W.A. Awards for
the Best Crime Novel
of 1964

Ross Macdonald
THE CHILL

'This author has got the Private Eye
novel off to perfection now, and
comparisons with Chandler and
Hammett have become superfluous
. . . Enormous quantities of plot, and
pages of imperceptibly witty dialogue
make this a very good bit of value for
money.'
Len Harris, Books and Bookmen

'Without, in the least abusing my
admiration for Dashiell Hammett and
Raymond Chandler, I should like to
venture the heretical suggestion that
Ross Macdonald is a better novelist
than either of them.'
Anthony Boucher, The New York Times
Book Review

Published for
The Crime Club
by Collins

Ross
Macdonald

'When it comes to Private Eyes Ross
Macdonald's Lew Archer is not only the
most intelligent of the lot, but he is
civilised and humane as well. He is
engaged in

THE FAR SIDE
OF THE DOLLAR

to find a boy who has broken out from
a school for the delinquent sons of
wealthy families and is met by a wall of
silence from everyone he questions.
Mr. Macdonald unravels the tangled plot
step by step. Without overdoing the
social criticism, he draws a bleak picture
of a society whose only values are
governed by the dollar.'
Violet Grant, Daily Telegraph

Ross
Mac-
donald

ROSS
MACDONALD

BLACK
money

BLACK
money

CRIME
CLUB
CHOICE

CRIME
CLUB
CHOICE

In what is perhaps his strangest
case Lew Archer, the celebrated
private-eye, explores the secret
life of a rich Californian residential
suburb. A beautiful young woman
has jilted her fiancé and taken up
with a mysterious character who
represents himself as a French
political refugee. Hired to
investigate this man Archer
becomes involved in several
murders and a gigantic swindle.

Running through the book, as a
central theme, is the corrupting
influence of the underworld and its
money on modern society.

Black Money is the most individual
of the brilliant series of novels that
have won Ross Macdonald
international recognition.

Dust jacket for A 20.2.a

A 21 THE INSTANT ENEMY

A 21.1.a
First edition, first printing (1968)

THE INSTANT ENEMY

Ross Macdonald

ALFRED · A · KNOPF New York 1968

A 21.1.a: 5⁹/₁₆″ × 8¹/₁₆″

THIS IS A BORZOI BOOK
PUBLISHED BY ALFRED A. KNOPF, INC.

FIRST EDITION

© Copyright 1968 by Ross Macdonald. All rights reserved under
International and Pan-American Copyright Conventions. Distributed
by Random House, Inc. Published simultaneously in Toronto,
Canada, by Random House of Canada Limited. Manufactured in
the United States of America.

Library of Congress Catalog Card Number: 68-12667

[i–viii] [1–3] 4–7 [8] 9–14 [15] 16–25 [26] 27–32 [33] 34–37 [38] 39–50 [51] 52–54
[55] 56–62 [63] 64–70 [71] 72–78 [79] 80–91 [92] 93–102 [103] 104–120 [121] 122–
127 [128] 129–136 [137] 138–150 [151] 152–169 [170] 171–227 [228–232]

[1–6]¹⁶ [7]⁸ [8]¹⁶

Contents: p. i: blank; p. ii: card page, 17 titles; p. iii: half title; p. iv: blank; p. v: title; p.
vi: copyright; p. vii: *'to Ping Ferry':* p. viii: blank; p. 1: half title; p. 2: blank; pp. 3–227:
text; p. 228: blank; p. 229: note on author; p. 230: note on type; pp. 231–232: blank.

Typography and paper: 6¹/₈″ (6⁵/₁₆″) × 3³/₄″. 36 or 37 lines per page. Running heads:
rectos only, 'THE INSTANT ENEMY'. Wove paper.

Binding: Three-piece binding: Dark yellow (#88) paper-covered boards with strong
greenish blue (#169) V-cloth (smooth) shelfback. Front blindstamped: 'R [typographi-
cal flower] M'. Spine silverstamped: '[rules and type decorations] | *The* | *Instant* |
Enemy | [rule] | Ross | Macdonald | [rules and type decorations] | *Knopf'.* Back:
blindstamped borzoi device. White endpapers. Top edge trimmed; bottom edge
rough-trimmed. Top edge stained greenish yellow.

Dust jacket: Front white; spine black; back white. Front lettered in green and black
with gray and pink art.

Publication: Published 12 February 1968. $4.50. Copyright #A 974759.

Printing: Composed, printed, and bound by Haddon Craftsmen, Scranton, Pa.

Locations: LC (FEB 13 1968); Lilly (dj); MJB (dj); UC-I (dj).

A 21.1.b
First edition, second printing: New York: Knopf, 1968.

Mystery Guild.

the instant enemy

ross macdonald

a new novel by the author of
"The Far Side of the Dollar" and "Black Money"

the instant enemy   ross macdonald

lew archer

is hired by Keith Sebastian, a Los Angeles business executive, to find his daughter Sandy, a high-school senior who has run off with a homeless boy. Sebastian and his wife, living on the edge of affluent bankruptcy, seem unable to communicate with their daughter. Archer finds the runaways easily enough, but before he can return Sandy to her parents, she has participated in a violent crime. Archer's efforts to save the girl from the consequences of her actions, and to understand these actions, involve him in a savage plot twisting deep into the past. At least one old murder and some new ones confront him and the police. Archer himself is very nearly killed by an ex-cop who wants to keep the case closed, but he finally manages to open it and let some daylight in. *The Instant Enemy* is Lew Archer at his toughest, and Ross Macdonald at his most trenchant in his observations of California society.

Jacket design by Muriel Liebson
2/68

ross macdonald

Photo Alfred A. Knopf

was born near San Francisco in 1915. He was educated in Canadian schools, traveled widely in Europe, and acquired advanced degrees and a Phi Beta Kappa key at the University of Michigan. In 1938 he married a Canadian girl who is now well known as the novelist Margaret Millar. Mr. Macdonald (Kenneth Millar in private life) taught school and later college, and served as Communications Officer aboard an escort carrier in the Pacific. For over twenty years he has lived in Santa Barbara and written mystery novels about the fascinating and changing society of his native state. Among his leading interests are conservation and politics. He is a past president of the Mystery Writers of America. In 1964 his novel *The Chill* was given a Silver Dagger award by the Crime Writers' Association of Great Britain. Mr. Macdonald's *The Far Side of the Dollar* was named the best crime novel of 1965 by the same organization. And *The Moving Target* was made into the highly successful movie *Harper* (1966).

Printed in U.S.A.

black money
(1966)

"Once more Macdonald scores highly; he has written no better book."
Harper's Monthly

"Mr. Macdonald some time ago passed the point where he merited consideration only as a creator of whodunits.... He is a serious novelist, all qualifications dismissed, with the serious novelist's duty to neither preach nor falsify."
Clifford A. Ridley, The National Observer

the far side of the dollar
(1965)

"Without in the least abating my admiration for Dashiell Hammett and Raymond Chandler, I should like to venture the heretical suggestion that Ross Macdonald is a better novelist than either of them."
Anthony Boucher, The New York Times Book Review

"Ross Macdonald is an important American novelist."
William Hogan, San Francisco Chronicle

Alfred · A · Knopf, Publisher, New York

Dust jacket for A 21.1.a

A 21.2
First English edition, only printing (1968)

THE
INSTANT ENEMY

by
ROSS MACDONALD

Published for

THE CRIME CLUB

by COLLINS, 14 ST JAMES'S PLACE
LONDON

A 21.2: $4^{15}/_{16}$″ × $7^{11}/_{16}$″

To
PING FERRY

© COPYRIGHT 1968 BY ROSS MACDONALD
PRINTED IN GREAT BRITAIN
COLLINS CLEAR-TYPE PRESS: LONDON AND GLASGOW

[1–4] 5–223 [224]

Perfect binding. Signed: [A]⁸ B–I⁸ K–O⁸

Contents: p. 1: blurb for *The Instant Enemy;* p. 2: card page, 15 titles; p. 3: title; p. 4: copyright and dedication; pp. 5–223: text; p. 224; ad for the Crime Club.

Typography and paper: 5³⁄₄″ (6″) × 3⁵⁄₈″. 37 or 38 lines per page. Wove paper.

Binding: Deep reddish orange (#36) paper-covered boards with V-pattern (smooth). Spine goldstamped: 'THE | INSTANT | ENEMY | ROSS | MACDONALD | [masked figure] | THE | CRIME | CLUB'. White endpapers. All edges trimmed.

Dust jacket: Front, back, and spine white. Front lettered in black, white, and pink with color photo.

Publication: 3,978 copies of the first printing. Published 12 August 1968. 18s.

Printing: See copyright page.

Locations: BL (19 JUL 68), MJB (dj).

A 21.3
Third edition: New York, Toronto, London: Bantam, [1969].

#H4405. Wrappers. 13 printings, 1969–1977.

A 21.4
Fourth edition: [London]: Fontana/Collins, [1970].

#2403. Wrappers. 6 printings, 1970–1980.

A 21.5
Fifth edition: Archer in Jeopardy. New York: Knopf, 1979.

Includes *The Instant Enemy.*

See AA 3.

A 21.6
Sixth edition: South Yarmouth, Mass.: John Curley, [1981].

Large-print edition. Wrappers.

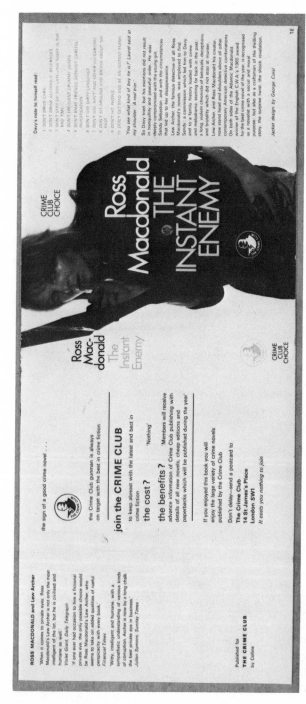

ROSS MACDONALD and Lew Archer

'When it comes to private eyes, Ross Macdonald's Lew Archer is not only the most intelligent of the lot, but he is civilised and humane as well.' *Violet Grant, Daily Telegraph*

'If one ever had occasion to hire a fictional private eye, the only possible choice would be Ross Macdonald's Lew Archer, who seems to take on added qualities of rueful perspicacity with every book.' *Financial Times*

'Witty, intelligent and humane, with a sympathetic understanding of various kinds of corruption, Archer is now by a long chalk the best private eye in business.' *Julian Symons, Sunday Times*

Published for
THE CRIME CLUB
by Collins

the sign of a good crime novel ...

the Crime Club gunman is always on target with the best in crime fiction

join the CRIME CLUB
to keep abreast with the latest and best in crime fiction

the cost? 'Nothing'

the benefits? 'Members will receive advance information of Crime Club publishing with details of all new novels, cheap editions and paperbacks which will be published during the year'

If you enjoyed this book you will enjoy the large variety of crime novels published by the Crime Club

Don't delay—send a postcard to
The Crime Club
14 St James's Place
London SW1
It costs you nothing to join

Ross Macdonald THE INSTANT ENEMY

CRIME CLUB CHOICE

Davy's note to himself read:

1 DON'T DRIVE CARS.
2 DON'T DRINK ALCOHOLIC BEVERAGES.
3 DON'T STAY UP TOO LATE—THE NIGHT IS THE BAD TIME.
4 DON'T FREQUENT CRUMBY JOINTS.
5 DON'T MAKE FRIENDS WITHOUT CAREFUL INVESTIGATION.
6 DON'T USE DIRTY LANGUAGE.
7 DON'T KILL ANYT AND OTHER HUMAN ONE.
8 DON'T SIT AROUND AND BROOD ABOUT THE PAST.
9 DON'T HIT PEOPLE.
10 DON'T GET MAD AND BE AN INSTANT ENEMY.

'*You see what kind of boy he is?*' Laurel said at my shoulder '*A real star.*'

So Davy tried but his exercises did not result in tranquility and peaceful order. He was deeply compromised with the young girl Sandy Sebastian, and with the circumstances that led up to her disappearance.

Lew Archer, the famous detective of all Ross Macdonald's novels, was employed to find Sandy, a commission which led him to Davy, and to a family history loaded with crime, and melodrama starting far back in the past, a long violent chronicle of betrayals, deceptions and brutality which did not stop at murder.

Lew Archer and Ross Macdonald his creator now stand head and shoulders above all other contemporary American detective combinations. On both sides of the Atlantic Macdonald, winner of the English C.W.A.'s 1965 award for the best crime novel of the year, is recognised as a novelist with a social and moral purpose: but also as a craftsman of the thrilling story, the surprise twist: the shock revelation.

Jacket design by George Coral

Dust jacket for A 21.2

A 22 THE GOODBYE LOOK

A 22.1.a
First edition, first printing (1969)

THE GOODBYE LOOK

ROSS MACDONALD

ALFRED · A · KNOPF
New York 1969

A 22.1.a: 5⁹/₁₆″ × 8″

THIS IS A BORZOI BOOK
PUBLISHED BY ALFRED A. KNOPF, INC.

First Edition
Copyright © 1969 by Ross Macdonald
All rights reserved under International and
Pan-American Copyright Conventions.
Published in the United States by
Alfred A. Knopf, Inc., New York, and simultaneously in
Canada by Random House of Canada Limited, Toronto.
Distributed by Random House, Inc., New York.
Library of Congress Catalog Card Number: 69-14735
Manufactured in the United States of America

[i–viii] [1–3] 4–243 [244–248]

[1–8]^{16}

Contents: p. i: blank; p. ii: card page, 18 titles; p. iii: half title; p. iv: blank; p. v: title; p. vi: copyright; p. vii: *'To Henri Coulette';* p. viii: blank; p. 1: half title; p. 2: blank; pp. 3–243: text; p. 244: blank; p. 245: note on author; p. 246: note on type; pp. 247–248: blank.

Typography and paper: 6^{1}/₁₆″ (6^{5}/₈″) × 3^{3}/₄″. 34 or 35 lines per page. Running heads: versos only, *'The Goodbye Look'.* Wove paper.

Binding: Three-piece binding: Black paper-covered boards with very reddish orange (#34) V-cloth (smooth) shelfback. Front blindstamped: '[type decorations] | RM | [type decorations]'. Spine goldstamped: '[rules and type decorations] | *The* | *Good-* | *bye* | *Look* | [type decoration] | Ross | Macdonald | [rules and type decorations] | KNOPF'. Back: blindstamped borzoi device. White endpapers. Top and bottom edges trimmed. Top edge stained strong red.

Dust jacket: Front, spine, and back yellow. Front lettered in red and black with black art.

Publication: 12,500 copies of the first printing. Published 28 May 1969. $4.95. Copyright #A 120679.

Printing: Composed, printed, and bound by Haddon Craftsmen, Scranton, Pa.

Locations: LC (DEC 18 1969); Lilly (dj); MJB (dj); UC-I (dj).

A 22.1.b
First edition, second printing: New York: Knopf, 1969.

A 22.1.c
First edition, third printing: New York: Knopf, 1969.

On copyright page: 'Third Printing, July 1969'.

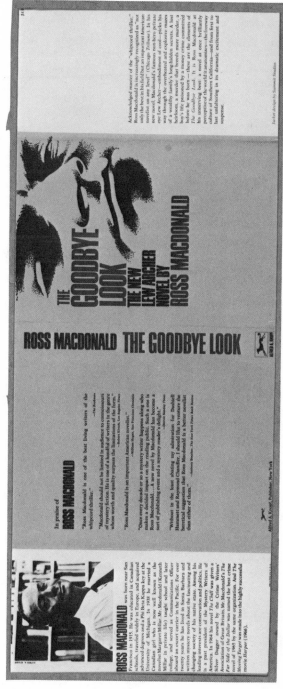

Dust jacket for A 22.1.a

A 22.1.d
First edition, fourth printing: New York: Knopf, 1969.

On copyright page: 'Fourth Printing, August 1969'.

A 22.1.e
First edition, fifth printing: New York: Knopf, 1969.

On coyright page: 'Fifth Printing, August 1969'.

A 22.1.f
First edition, sixth printing: New York: Knopf, 1969.

On copyright page: 'Sixth Printing, September 1969'.

Also distributed by the Literary Guild.

A 22.1.g
First edition, seventh printing: New York: Knopf, 1969.

On copyright page: 'Seventh Printing, October 1969'.

A 22.1.h
First edition, eighth printing: New York: Knopf, 1969.

On copyright page: 'Eighth Printing, October 1969'.

A 22.2
Second edition: New York: Knopf, 1969.

[i–vi] 1–215 [216–218]. Reprinted 1972.

Mystery Guild.

A 22.3.a
First English edition, first printing (1969)

THE GOODBYE LOOK

by

ROSS MACDONALD

Published for

THE CRIME CLUB

by COLLINS, 14 ST JAMES'S PLACE
LONDON

A 22.3.a: 4¹⁵/16″ × 7¹¹/16″

[1–4] 5–223 [224]

Perfect binding. Signed: [A]⁸ B–I⁸ [K]⁸ L–O⁸

Contents: p. 1: blurb for *The Goodbye Look;* p. 2: card page, 16 titles; p. 3: title; p. 4: copyright; pp. 5–223: text; p. 224: blank.

Typography and paper: 6″ (6³/₁₆″) × 3⁵/₈″. 38 lines per page. No running heads. Wove paper.

Binding: Deep reddish orange (#36) paper-covered boards with V-pattern (smooth). Spine goldstamped: 'THE | GOODBYE | LOOK | Ross | Macdonald | [within circle] [masked figure] THE CRIME CLUB'. White endpapers. All edges trimmed.

Dust jacket: Front and spine black; back white. Front lettered in white and green with color photo.

Publication: Published 25 August 1969. 21s.

Printing: See copyright page.

Locations: Lilly (dj); MJB (dj); UC-I (dj).

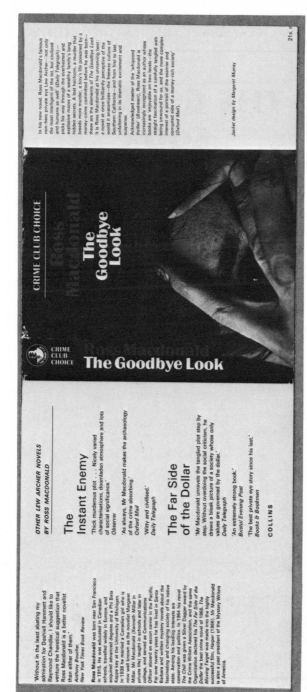

CRIME CLUB CHOICE

Ross Macdonald

The Goodbye Look

CRIME CLUB CHOICE

Ross Macdonald

The Goodbye Look

OTHER LEW ARCHER NOVELS
BY ROSS MACDONALD

The Instant Enemy

'Thick murderous plot . . . Nicely varied characterisations, doomladen atmosphere and lots of social significance.'
Observer

'As always, Mr Macdonald makes the archaeology of the crime absorbing.'
Oxford Mail

'Witty and civilised.'
Daily Telegraph

The Far Side of the Dollar

'Mr Macdonald unravels the tangled plot step by step. Without overdoing the social criticism, he draws a bleak picture of a society whose only values are governed by the dollar.'
Daily Telegraph

'An extremely strong book.'
Bristol Evening Post

'The best private eye story since his last.'
Books & Bookmen

COLLINS

Dust jacket for A 22.3.a

A 22.3.b
First English edition, second printing: London: Thriller Book Club, [1970].

THE GOODBYE LOOK

by
ROSS MACDONALD

THRILLER BOOK CLUB
121 CHARING CROSS ROAD
LONDON, w.c.2.

A 22.3.b: 4^{11}/$_{16}$″ × 7^{3}/$_{16}$″

A 22.4
Fourth edition: New York, Toronto, London: Bantam, [1970].

#N5357. Wrappers. 10 printings, 1970–1977.

A 22.5
Fifth edition: [London]: Fontana/Collins, [1970].

#2404. Wrappers. Reprinted 1972, 1974, 1978.

A 22.6
Sixth edition: Boston: G. K. Hall, 1972.

Large-type edition.

A 22.7
Seventh edition: A Treasury of Modern Mysteries. Garden City, N.Y.: Doubleday, [1973].

Volume 1 includes *The Goodbye Look.*

A 23 *THE UNDERGROUND MAN*

A 23.1.a
First edition, first printing (1971)

THE

UNDERGROUND

MAN

ᴐᴐᴐᴐᴐᴐᴐᴐᴐᴐᴐᴐ

R O S S   M A C D O N A L D

ᴐᴐᴐᴐᴐᴐᴐᴐᴐᴐᴐᴐ

Alfred A. Knopf · New York · 1971

A 23.1.a: 5^{11}/₁₆″ × 8^{5}/₁₆″

THIS IS A BORZOI BOOK
PUBLISHED BY ALFRED A. KNOPF, INC.

Copyright © 1971 by Ross Macdonald
All rights reserved under International
and Pan-American Copyright Conventions.
Published in the United States by
Alfred A. Knopf, Inc., New York,
and simultaneously in Canada by
Random House of Canada Limited, Toronto.
Distributed by Random House, Inc., New York.
Library of Congress Catalog Card Number: 76-136337
Standard Book Number: 0-394-43467-6
Manufactured in the United States of America.

FIRST EDITION

[i–viii] [1–2] 3–272 [273–280]

[1–9]^{16}

Contents: p. i: blank; p. ii: card page, 19 titles; p. iii: half title; p. iv: blank; p. v: title; p. vi: copyright; p. vii: 'To | Matthew J. *Bruccoli*'; p. viii: blank; p. 1: half title; p. 2: blank; pp. 3–273: text; p. 274: blank; p. 275: note on author; p. 276: blank; p. 277: note on type; pp. 278–280: blank.

Typography and paper: 6^3/$_8$″ (6^{15}/$_{16}$″) × 3^3/$_4$″. 34 lines per page. Running heads: versos only, '*The Underground Man*'. Wove paper.

Binding: Three-piece binding: Strong orange (#50) paper-covered boards with black V-cloth (smooth) shelfback. Front blindstamped: '[type decoration] | RM | [type decoration]'. Spine goldstamped: '[type decorations] | *The* | *Under-* | *ground* | *Man* | [line of wavy dashes and dots] | ROSS | MACDONALD | [type decorations] | KNOPF'. White endpapers. Top and bottom edges trimmed. Top edge stained black.

Dust jacket: Front, spine, and back orange. Front lettered in purple, black, and white with art in black and white on purple panel.

Publication: 20,000 copies of the first printing. Published 19 February 1971. $5.95. Copyright #A 247417. ISBN: 0-394-43467-6.

Printing: Composed, printed, and bound by Haddon Craftsmen, Scranton, Pa.

Locations: LC (JUN 15 1971); Lilly (dj); MJB (dj); UC-I (dj).

A 23.1.b
First edition, second printing: New York: Knopf, 1971.

On copyright page: 'FIRST AND SECOND PRINTING BEFORE PUBLICATION'.

A 23.1.c
First edition, third printing. New York: Knopf, 1971.

On copyright page: 'THIRD PRINTING, FEBRUARY 1971'.

A 23.1.d
First edition, fourth printing: New York: Knopf, 1971.

On copyright page: 'FOURTH PRINTING, MARCH 1971'.

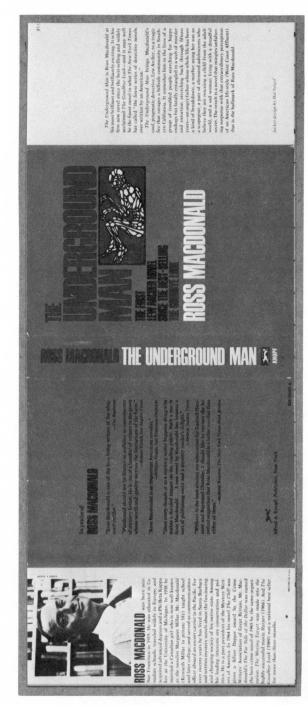

Dust jacket for A 23.1.a

A 23.1.e
First edition, fifth printing: New York: Knopf, 1971.

On copyright page: 'FIFTH PRINTING, APRIL 1971'. Sheets of the fifth printing were distributed by the Book-of-the-Month Club.

A 23.1.f
First edition, sixth printing: New York: Knopf, 1971.

On copyright page: 'SIXTH PRINTING, MAY 1971'.

A 23.1.g
First edition, pirated reprints: New York: Knopf, 1971.

Probably printed in Taiwan. Noted with and without Chinese type on copyright page. *Location:* MJB (both).

A 23.2.a
First English edition, first printing (1971)

The Underground Man

Ross Macdonald

The Crime Club
Collins, 14 St James's Place, London

A 23.2.a: 4^{15}/$_{16}$″ × 7^{3}/$_{4}$″

William Collins Sons & Co Ltd
London · Glasgow · Sydney · Auckland
Toronto · Johannesburg

First published in Great Britain 1971

© Ross Macdonald, 1971

ISBN 0 00 231848 8

Set in Intertype Baskerville
Made and Printed in Great Britain by
William Collins Sons & Co Ltd Glasgow

[1–7] 8–255 [256]

Perfect binding. Signed: [A]^8 B–I^8 K–Q^8

Contents: p. 1: blurb for *The Underground Man;* p. 2: card page, 16 titles; p. 3: title; p. 4: copyright; p. 5: dedication; p. 6: blank; pp. 7–255: text; p. 256: blank.

Typography and paper: 5³/₄″ (6″) × 3¹¹/₁₆″. 35 or 36 lines per page. Running heads: rectos and versos, 'THE UNDERGROUND MAN'. Wove paper.

Binding: Deep reddish-orange (#36) paper-covered boards with V-pattern (smooth). Spine goldstamped: 'THE | UNDER- | GOUND | MAN | ROSS | MACDONALD | [within circle] [masked figure] THE CRIME CLUB'. White endpapers. All edges trimmed.

Dust jacket: Front and spine green and brown; back white. Front lettered in white and black with yellow, black, and brown art.

Publication: Published 1 November 1971. £1.50.

Printing: See copyright page.

Locations: BL (22 OCT 71); Lilly (dj); MJB (dj); UC-I (dj).

A 23.2.b
First English edition, second printing: London: Book Club Associates, [1972].

MJB (dj).

A 23.3
Third edition: The Case of the Fabulous Fake | El Rancho Rio | The Underground Man. Roslyn, N.Y.: Detective Book Club, [1971].

A 23.4
Fourth edition: Boston: G. K. Hall, 1971.

Large-type edition. Two printings.

A 23.5
Fifth edition: London: Odhams, 1972.

Not seen.

Dust jacket for A 23.2.a

A 23.6
Sixth edition: New York, Toronto, London: Bantam, [1972].

#Q7040. Wrappers. 350,000 copies. 14 printings, 1972–1979.

A 23.7
Seventh edition: [London]: Fontana/Collins, [1973].

#2850. Wrappers. Reprinted 1973, 1974, 1977.

Note: Condensed in *Cosmopolitan* 170 (February 1971), 172–176, 178, 180, 184, 186–190, 192, 194–204.

A 24 SLEEPING BEAUTY

A 24.1.a
First edition, first printing (1973)

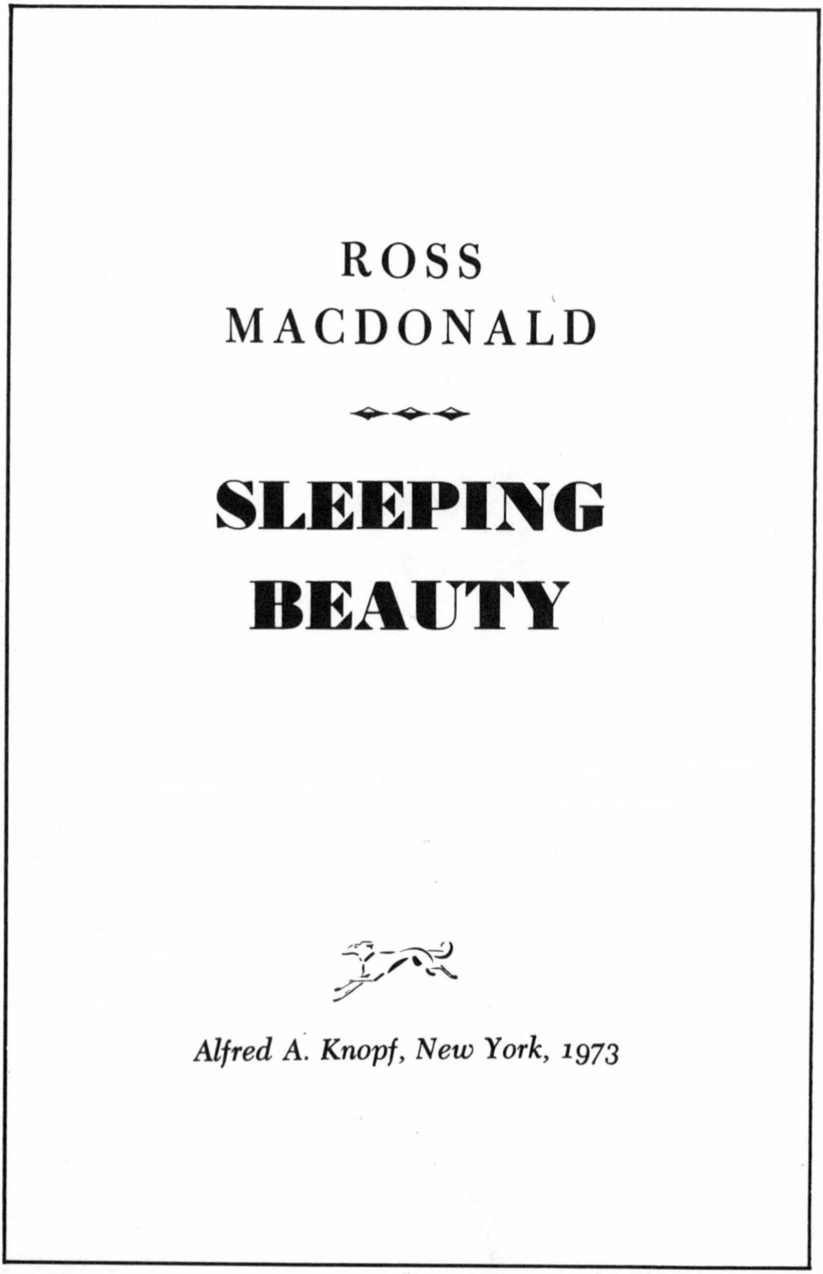

ROSS
MACDONALD

❖❖❖

SLEEPING

BEAUTY

Alfred A. Knopf, New York, 1973

A 24.1.a: $5^5/8''$ × $8^1/4''$

THIS IS A BORZOI BOOK
PUBLISHED BY ALFRED A. KNOPF, INC.

Copyright © 1973 by Ross Macdonald.
All rights reserved under International and
Pan-American Copyright Conventions. Published
in the United States by Alfred A. Knopf, Inc.,
New York, and simultaneously in Canada by
Random House of Canada Limited, Toronto.
Distributed by Random House, Inc., New York.

Library of Congress Cataloging in Publication Data
————. Sleeping beauty.
I. Title.
PZ3.M59943Sl [PS3525.I486] 813'.5'2 72–11037
ISBN 0–394–48474–6

Manufactured in the United States of America
FIRST EDITION

[i–x] [1–3] 4–11 [12] 13–23 [24] 25–57 [58] 59–78 [79] 80–88 [89] 90–156 [157] 158–180 [181] 182–184 [185] 186–213 [214] 215–271 [272–278]

[1–9]¹⁶

Contents: pp. i–iii: blank; p. iv: card page, 20 titles; p. v: half title; p. vi: blank; p. vii: title; p. viii: copyright; p. ix: dedication; p. x: blank; p. 1: half title; p. 2: blank; pp. 3–271: text; p. 272: blank; p. 273: note on author; p. 274: blank; p. 275: note on type; pp. 276–278: blank.

Typography and paper: 6⁷/₁₆″ (6¹¹/₁₆″) × 4¹/₁₆″. 35 lines per page. Running heads: versos only, *'Sleeping Beauty'*. Wove paper.

Binding: Dark purplish blue (#201) V-cloth (smooth). Front blindstamped: '[type decoration] | RM | [type decoration]'. Spine goldstamped: '[type decoration] | *Sleeping | Beauty* | [line of diamonds] | ROSS | MACDONALD | [type decoration] | KNOPF'. Back: blindstamped borzoi device. White endpapers. Top edge trimmed; bottom edge rough-trimmed. Top edge stained strong purplish pink.

Dust jacket: Front and spine blue; back white. Front lettered in orange, pink, and white with art in white and blue on multicolored rectangle.

Publication: 35,000 copies of the first printing. Published 9 May 1973. $5.95. Copyright #A 453029. ISBN: 0-394-48474-6.

Printing: Composed, printed, and bound by Haddon Craftsmen, Scranton, Pa.

Locations: LC (AUG 6 1973); Lilly (dj); MJB (dj); UC-I (dj).

A 24.1.b
First edition, second printing: New York: Knopf, 1973.

On copyright page. 'FIRST AND SECOND PRINTINGS BEFORE PUBLICATION'.

A 24.1.c
First edition, third printing: New York: Knopf, 1973.

Not seen.

Dust jacket for A 24.1.a

A 24.1.d
First edition, fourth printing: New York: Knopf, 1973.

On copyright page: 'FOURTH PRINTING, JULY 1973'.

A 24.1.e
First edition, pirated reprint: New York: Knopf, 1973.

Probably printed in Taiwan. Not seen.

A 24.2.a
Second edition, first printing: New York: Knopf, [1973].

[i–vi] [1]–280 [281–282].

Mystery Guild. Also distributed by Literary Guild.

A 24.3.a
First English edition, first printing (1973)

Sleeping Beauty

Ross Macdonald

The Crime Club
Collins, 14 St James's Place, London

A 24.3.a: 5″ × 7⁵/₈″

William Collins Sons & Co Ltd
London · Glasgow · Sydney · Auckland
Toronto · Johannesburg

First published in Great Britain 1973
© Ross Macdonald, 1973
ISBN 0 00 231775 3
Set in Monotype Imprint
Made and Printed in Great Britain by
William Collins Sons & Co Ltd Glasgow

[1–7] 8–253 [254–256]

Perfect binding. Signed: [A]⁸ B–I⁸ K–Q⁸

Contents: p. 1: blurb for *Sleeping Beauty;* p. 2: card page, 17 titles; p. 3: title; p. 4: copyright; p. 5: dedication; p. 6: blank; pp. 7–253: text; pp. 254–256: blank.

Typography and paper: $5^{15}/_{16}''$ ($6^1/_8''$) × $3^{11}/_{16}''$. 39 lines per page. Running heads: rectos and versos, 'SLEEPING BEAUTY'. Wove paper.

Binding: Deep reddish orange (#36) paper-covered boards with V-pattern (smooth). Spine goldstamped: 'Sleeping | Beauty | Ross | Macdonald | [within circle] [masked figure] | THE CRIME CLUB'. White endpapers. All edges trimmed.

Dust jacket: Front and spine black and blue; back white. Front lettered in red and white with color photo of capsules and container.

Publication: Published 17 September 1973. £1.70.

Printing: See copyright page.

Locations: BL (4 SEP 73); Lilly (dj); MJB (dj); UC-I(dj).

Proof copy: First printing sheets bound in unprinted reddish orange wrappers. *Location:* MJB.

A 24.3.b
First English edition, second printing: London: Book Club Associates, 1973.

Not seen.

A 24.4
Fourth edition: Boston: G. K. Hall, 1973.

Large-type edition.

A 24.5
Fifth edition: New York, Toronto, London: Bantam, [1974].

#T8254. Wrappers.

A 24.6
Sixth edition: [London]: Fontana/Collins, [1975].

#3964. Wrappers.

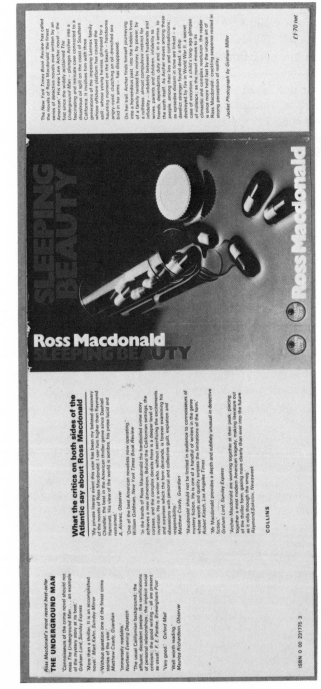

Dust jacket for A 24.3:a

A 25 ON CRIME WRITING

A 25.1.a
First edition, first printing, limited issue (1973)

Number Eleven - Yes! Capra Chapbook Series

Ross Macdonald

On Crime Writing

THE WRITER AS DETECTIVE HERO

WRITING THE GALTON CASE

CAPRA PRESS   1973   SANTA BARBARA

A 25.1.a: 5″ × 7″. Top and bottom lines and decorations in red.

[i–iv] v–vii [viii] 9–45 [46–48]

[1–3]^8

Contents: p. i: list of 12 Capra chapbooks; p. ii: blank; p. iii: title; p. iv: copyright; pp. v–vii: foreword; p. viii: 'for Donald Davie'; pp. 9–24: 'The Writer As | Detective Hero'; pp. 25–45: 'Writing The | Galton Case'; p. 46: blank; p. 47: certificate of limitation '[goat] | *This chapbook series, edited by Robert Durand | (YES! PRESS) and Noel Young (CAPRA PRESS), is | designed and printed by Capra Press in Santa | Barbara. This is the eleventh title in the series, | published July 1973. | Two hundred and fifty numbered | copies, signed by the author, were handbound'.* See B 10, C 138.

Typography and paper: 4^{15}/₁₆″ (5^5/₁₆″) × 3⅝″. 25 lines per page. No running heads. Wove paper.

Binding: White paper-covered boards. Front: 'ON CRIME WRITING | ROSS MACDON-ALD | [bisected portrait of Macdonald | Archer] | [deep yellow (#85)] [type decoration] YES! CAPRA CHAPBOOK SERIES [type decoration] | ROSS MACDONALD LEW ARCHER'. Spine: '[vertically] [medium gray (#265) rules and decoration] [black] ROSS MACDONALD—ON CRIME WRITING YES! CAPRA CHAPBOOK SERIES [medium gray rules and decoration]'. Back: medium gray decorations. Strong red (#12) endpapers. All edges trimmed.

Dust jacket: Published without dust jacket.

Publication: Limited and trade issues published simultaneously. Published July 1973. 250 numbered copies. $10. ISBN: 0-912264-67-5.

Printing: See certificate of limitation.

Locations: Lilly; MJB; UC-I

A 25.1.a*
First edition, first printing, trade issue (1973)

Title page, pagination, collation, typography, paper, and contents same as limited issue.

Binding: Paper wrappers same as boards binding of limited issue, with addition of '$2.50' on back wrapper. Color of last two lines on front cover is very reddish orange (#34).

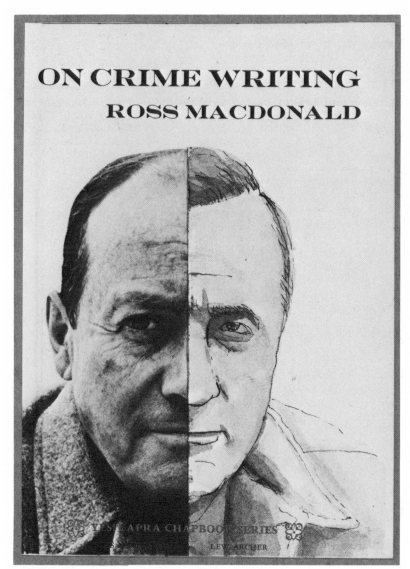

ON CRIME WRITING

ROSS MACDONALD

Front cover for A 25.1.a

Publication: 2,500 copies. $1.95. ISBN: 0-912264-66-7.

Locations: LC (29 APR 75 CIP); MJB.

A 25.1.b
First edition, second printing: Santa Barbara, Cal.: Capra Press, 1973.

Title page printed in black; otherwise undifferentiated from first printing, trade issue.

A 26 GREAT STORIES OF SUSPENSE

A 26.1.a
First edition, first printing (1974)

GREAT STORIES
OF SUSPENSE

edited by

ROSS MACDONALD

Alfred A. Knopf / New York / 1974

A 26.1.a: 6^{1}/$_{16}$″ × 9^{3}/$_{16}$″

THIS IS A BORZOI BOOK
PUBLISHED BY ALFRED A. KNOPF, INC.

Copyright © 1974 by Alfred A. Knopf, Inc.

All rights reserved under International and Pan-American Copyright Conventions. Published in the United States by Alfred A. Knopf, Inc., New York,
and simultaneously in Canada by Random House of Canada Limited, Toronto.
Distributed by Random House, Inc., New York.

LIBRARY OF CONGRESS CATALOGING IN PUBLICATION DATA

Macdonald, Ross, Date comp.
Great stories of suspense.
CONTENTS: Collier, J. Wet Saturday.—Fearing, K. The big clock.
—Christie, A. What Mrs. McGillicuddy saw! [etc.]
1. Detective and mystery stories, American.
2. Detective and mystery stories, English. I. Title.
PZ1.M146Gr [PS648.D4]   823'.0872   74-7743
ISBN 0-394-49292-7

Manufactured in the United States of America

FIRST EDITION

Grateful acknowledgment is given for permission to reprint previously published material:

WET SATURDAY, John Collier. Reprinted by permission of The Harold Mat-
son Company, Inc. Originally published in *The New Yorker*. Copyright © 1966
by John Collier.
THE BIG CLOCK, Kenneth Fearing. Reprinted by permission of Russell &
Volkening, Inc. Copyright 1946 by Kenneth Fearing and renewed 1974 by
Bruce Fearing.
WHAT MRS. MCGILLICUDDY SAW!, Agatha Christie. Reprinted by permis-
sion of Dodd, Mead & Company, Inc., and William Collins Sons & Company
Ltd. Copyright © 1957 by Agatha Christie Ltd.
THE PAYOFF, Stanley Ellin. Reprinted by permission of Curtis Brown Ltd.
Originally published in *Ellery Queen's Mystery Magazine*. Copyright © 1971
by Stanley Ellin.

[a–b] [i–ix] x–xvii [xviii] [1–3] 4–823 [824–828]. First page of each selection unnum-
bered.

[1–11]^{32} [12–13]^{16} [14]^8 [15]^{32}

Contents: pp. a–b: blank; p. i: half title; p. ii: blank; p. iii: title; pp. iv–v: copyright; p.
vi: blank: p. vii: contents; p. viii: blank; p. ix–xvii: introduction by Ross Macdonald; p. 1:
half title; p. 2: blank; pp. 3–823: text; p. 824: blank; p. 825: note on editor; p. 826:
blank; p. 827: note on type; p. 828: blank.

Includes "Wet Saturday" by John Collier, *The Big Clock* by Kenneth Fearing, *What
Mrs. McGillicuddy Saw!* by Agatha Christie, "The Payoff" by Stanley Ellin, "The Base-
ment Room" by Graham Greene, "Fly Paper" by Dashiell Hammett, "The Five-Forty-
Eight" by John Cheever, *The Strange Case of Dr. Jekyll and Mr. Hyde* by Robert Louis
Stevenson, "The Baby in the Icebox" by James M. Cain, "The Couple Next Door" by
Margaret Millar, "The Landlady" by Roald Dahl, "The Amateur" by Michael Gilbert,
"The Terrapin" by Patricia Highsmith, *Enquiry* by Dick Francis, *The Far Side of the
Dollar* by Ross Macdonald, "The Comforts of Home" by Flannery O'Connor. See A 19.

Typography and paper: 7^9/₁₆″ (7^7/₈″) × 4^3/₈″. 44 lines per page. Running heads: rectos, title of selection; versos, author's name. Wove paper.

Binding: Black V-cloth (smooth). Front blindstamped with ladder-like design. Spine silverstamped: '[design of decorated rectangles] | GREAT | STORIES | OF | SUSPENSE | [design of decorated rectangles] | *edited by* Ross | Macdonald | *Alfred A. Knopf* | [design of decorated rectangles]'. Blindstamped rectangular borzoi device on back. Off-white endpapers. All edges trimmed. Top edge stained purplish pink.

Dust jacket: Black; front lettered in pink, red and white with woman's face in white vertical lines.

Publication: 10,000 copies of the first printing. Published 18 November 1974. $12.50. Copyright #A 608751. ISBN: 0-394-49292-7.

Printing: Composed by Haddon Craftsmen, Scranton, Pa.; printed and bound by the Book Press, Brattleboro, Vt.

Locations: LC (FEB 14 1975; 25 NOV 1974 CIP); Lilly (dj); MJB (dj); UC-I(dj).

A 26.1.b
First edition, Book-of-the-Month Club printing: New York: Knopf, 1974.

[1–25]^{16} [26]^{8} [27]^{16}

Dust jacket for A 26.1.a

A 27 THE BLUE HAMMER

A 27.1.a
First edition, first printing (1976)

THE BLUE HAMMER

❖❖❖❖❖❖❖❖❖❖❖❖

ROSS MACDONALD

Alfred A. Knopf, New York, 1976

A 27.1.a: 5^{11}/$_{16}$″ × 8^1/$_4$″

[i–viii] [1–3] 4–22 [23] 24–32 [33] 34–38 [39] 40–51 [52] 53–82 [83] 84–114 [115] 116–136 [137] 138–142 [143] 144–154 [155] 156–161 [162] 163–169 [170] 171–229 [230] 231–252 [253] 254–270 [271–280]

Gatherings glued, not sewn. Unsigned.

Contents: p. i: blank; p. ii: card page, 22 titles; p. iii: half title; p. iv: blank; p. v: title; p. vi: copyright; p. vii: '*To William Campbell Gault*'; p. viii: blank; p. 1: half title; p. 2: blank; pp. 3–270: text; pp. 271–272: blank; p. 273: note on author; p. 274: blank; p. 275: note on type; pp. 276–280: blank.

Typography and paper: 6⅞" (7⅛") × 4". 37 lines per page. Running heads: versos only, '*The Blue Hammer*'. Wove paper.

Binding: Three-piece binding: Brilliant Blue (#177) paper-covered boards with ripple pattern and black V-cloth (smooth) shelfback. Front blindstamped: '[type decoration] | RM | [type decoration]'. Spine goldstamped: '[lines of diamonds and type decoration] | *The* | *Blue* | *Hammer* | [line of diamonds] | ROSS MACDONALD | [lines of diamonds and type decorations] | KNOPF'. Back has blindstamped borzoi device. Yellowish white endpapers. Top edge trimmed; bottom edge rough trimmed. Green and yellow headbands and footbands. Top edge stained yellow.

Dust jacket: Front and spine white; back has black and white photo of Macdonald. Front lettered in blue, green and black with art in blue, green, yellow, and black.

$7.95

The theft of a valuable painting. The long-ago disappearance of a famous artist. A murder as deceptive as a magician's illusion. A breviation—but now buried-explosion of family hatred.

These are the nerve centers of Ross Macdonald's magnificent new Lew Archer novel, the richest we have had from the author of "the best detective novel ever written by an American" (The New York Times)—a fusion of unfaltering suspense with dramatic revelation of the way lives are shaped and mis-shaped in the flow of time, in the hidden and dangerous emotional currents beneath the surface of family history.

The time is now; the place, Southern California. The stolen canvas that Archer has been hired to retrieve is reputed to be the work of the celebrated Richard Chantry, who vanished in 1950 from his home in Santa Teresa. It is the portrait of an unknown woman—and on its trail Archer moves with edgy competence among the antiques of dealers and collectors. Until suddenly he finds himself drawn into a web of family complications and masked hostilities stretching back fifty years through a world where money talks or buys silence, where behind the plausible facades of homes not quite broken but badly bent, a heritage of lies and evasions pushes troubled men and women deeper into trouble. And as he pursues the Chantry portrait—and the larger mystery of Richard Chantry—Archer himself is shaken as never before. Archer the solitary traveler, the loner who has through the years deliberately addressed himself to the deciphering of other people's lives, is thrust into an inescapable encounter with a woman who will complicate his own.

From its almost hushed beginning to its violent climax and its unexpected—indeed astonishing

(continued on back flap)

THE BLUE HAMMER
THE NEW LEW ARCHER NOVEL BY ROSS MACDONALD

THE BLUE HAMMER ROSS MACDONALD

Knopf

JILL KREMENTZ

(continued from front flap)

ing-resolution, The Blue Hammer holds us riveted. This is Ross Macdonald at his incomparable best.

ROSS MACDONALD was born near San Francisco in 1915. He was educated in Canadian schools, traveled widely in Europe, and acquired advanced degrees and a Phi Beta Kappa key at the University of Michigan. In 1938 he married a Canadian who is now well known as the novelist Margaret Millar. Mr. Macdonald (Kenneth Millar in private life) taught school and later college, and served as communications officer aboard an escort carrier in the Pacific. For nearly thirty years he has lived in Santa Barbara and written mystery novels about the fascinating and changing society of his native state. Among his leading interests are conservation and politics. He is a past president of the Mystery Writers of America. In 1964 his novel The Chill was given a Silver Dagger award by the Crime Writers' Association of Great Britain. Mr. Macdonald's The Far Side of the Dollar was named the best crime novel of 1965 by the same organization. The Moving Target was made into the highly successful movie Harper (1966). And The Goodbye Look (1969), The Underground Man (1971), and Sleeping Beauty (1973) were all national best sellers.

Jacket design by Hal Siegel

Alfred A. Knopf, Publisher, New York
6/76

Dust jacket for A 27.1.a

Publication: 35,000 copies of the first printing. Published 15 June 1976. $7.95. Copyright #A 794282. ISBN: 0-394-40425-4.

Printing: Composed by Datagraphics, Phoenix, Ariz.; printed and bound by American Book–Stratford Press, Saddle Brook, N.J.

Locations: LC (NOV 2 1976); Lilly (dj); MJB (dj); UC-I(dj).

Proof copies: First printing sheets in greenish-yellow wrappers. Printed in black on front: 'THIS IS AN UNCORRECTED PROOF. | It should not be quoted without comparison | with the finally revised text. | THE | BLUE | HAMMER | [line of diamonds] | ROSS | MACDONALD | [borzoi] | *Alfred A. Knopf, New York, 1976*'.

Also with xeroxed publication information taped over front wrapper. Manufactured by Crane Duplicating Service, Barnstable, Mass. *Location:* MJB (both).

A 27.1.b
First edition, second printing: New York: Knopf, 1976.

On copyright page: 'Second Printing Before Publication'.

A 27.1.c
First edition, third printing: New York: Knopf, 1976.

On copyright page: 'Third Printing, July 1976'.

A 27.2
Second edition: New York: Knopf, [1976].

[i–vi] [1]–218

Mystery Guild.

A 27.3.a
Third edition, first printing: Boston: G. K. Hall, 1976.

Large-type edition.

A 27.3.b
Third edition, second printing: Boston & London: G. K. Hall & George Prior, [   ].

Not seen.

A 27.4.a
First English edition, first printing (1976)

The Blue Hammer

Ross Macdonald

A Lew Archer Novel

The Crime Club

Collins, 14 St James's Place, London

A 27.4.a: 5^1/$_8$″ × 7^3/$_4$″

To William Campbell Gault

William Collins Sons & Co Ltd
London · Glasgow · Sydney · Auckland
Toronto · Johannesburg
First published 1976
© 1976 by Ross Macdonald
ISBN 0 00 231049 X
Set in Monotype Baskerville
Made and printed in Great Britain by
William Collins Sons & Co Ltd Glasgow

[1–5] 6–256

Perfect binding. Signed: [A]–I K–Q^8

Contents: p. 1: blurb for *The Blue Hammer;* p. 2: card page, 18 titles; p. 3: title; p. 4: dedication and copyright; pp. 5–256: text.

Typography and paper: $5^{15}/_{16}''$ ($6^1/_8''$) × $3^5/_8''$. 38 or 39 lines per page. Running heads: rectos and versos, 'THE BLUE HAMMER'. Wove paper.

Binding: Deep reddish orange (#36) paper-covered boards with V-pattern (smooth). Spine goldstamped: 'THE | BLUE | HAMMER | Ross | Macdonald | [within circle] [masked figure] | THE CRIME CLUB'. White endpapers. All edges trimmed.

Dust jacket: Front and spine black; back white. Front lettered in blue, orange, and white with photo of broken palette.

Publication: Published 16 September 1976. £2.95.

Printing: See copyright page.

Locations: Lilly (dj); MJB (dj); UC-I(dj).

THE BLUE HAMMER

A new Lew Archer novel

Ross Macdonald

THE BLUE HAMMER
Ross Macdonald

CRIME CLUB CHOICE

The Author

Ross Macdonald was born near San Francisco in 1915. He was educated in Canadian schools, travelled widely in Europe, and acquired advanced degrees at the University of Michigan. In 1938 he married a Canadian who is now well known as the novelist Margaret Millar. Mr Macdonald (Kenneth Millar in private life) taught school and later college, and served as communications officer aboard an escort carrier in the Pacific. For nearly thirty years he has lived in Santa Barbara and written mystery novels about the fascinating and changing society of his native state. Among his leading interests are conservation and politics. He is a past president of the Mystery Writers of America. In 1964 his novel *The Chill* was given a Silver Dagger award by the Crime Writers' Association of Great Britain. Mr Macdonald's *The Far Side of the Dollar* was named the best crime novel of 1965 by the same organization. *The Moving Target* was made into the highly successful movie *Harper* (1966). And *The Goodbye Look* (1969), *The Underground Man* (1971) and *Sleeping Beauty* (1973) were also best sellers.

Jacket photograph by Derrick Witty
ISBN 0 00 231049 X

From the author of 'the best detective novels written by an American' *New York Times*

Ross Macdonald
SLEEPING BEAUTY

'The excellence of Mr Macdonald's sparse clear writing puts him in a class by himself at the top of the hardboiled naturalistic school.'
Maurice Richardson, Observer

'Genuine suspenseful, last page knockout murder mystery.'
Francis Goff, Sunday Telegraph

'Splendidly human private eye Lew Archer finds himself involved this time in the disappearance of a kooky oil heiress that sets all the family skeletons rattling. As usual Mr Macdonald offers much more than a mere mystery.'
Graham Lord, Sunday Express

'His seventeenth detective novel . . . each one is better than the last.'
Daily Mirror

'Dovetailed plotting, like the characterization, absorbing.'
Alec Spokesman, Northern Echo

'Compulsive reading.'
Oxford Mail

COLLINS

The theft of a valuable painting. The long-ago disappearance of a famous artist. A murder as deceptive as a magician's illusion. A horrendous - but now buried - explosion of family hatred.

These are the nerve centres of Ross Macdonald's new Lew Archer novel, the richest we have had from the author of the best detective novels ever written by an American' (*New York Times*) - a fusion of unflinching suspense with dramatic revelation of the way lives are shaped and mishaped in the flow of time, in the hidden and dangerous emotional currents beneath the surface of family history.

The time is now, the place. Southern California. The stolen canvas that Archer has been hired to retrieve is reputed to be the work of the celebrated Richard Chantry, who vanished in 1950 from his home in Santa Teresa. It is the portrait of an unknown woman - and on its trail Archer moves with edgy competence among the intrigues of dealers and collectors. Until suddenly he is drawn into a web of family complications and masked brutalities stretching back fifty years through a world where money talks or buys silence, where social prominence is a murderous weapon, where behind the plausible facades of homes not quite broken but badly bent, a heritage of lies and evasions pushes troubled men and women deeper into trouble. And as he pursues the Chantry portrait - and the larger mystery of Richard Chantry - Archer himself is shaken as never before: Archer, the solitary traveller, the loner who has through the years deliberately addressed himself to the deciphering of other people's lives, is thrust into an inescapable encounter with a woman who will complicate his own.

From its almost hushed beginning to its violent climax and unexpected - indeed astonishing - resolution, *The Blue Hammer* holds us riveted. This is Ross Macdonald at his incomparable best.

£2.95 NET

Dust jacket for A 27.4.a

A 27.4.b
First English edition, second printing: London: Book Club Associates, [1976].

The Blue Hammer

Ross Macdonald

A Lew Archer Novel

BOOK CLUB ASSOCIATES
LONDON

A 27.4.b: $5^3/_{16}$″ × $7^{11}/_{16}$″

A 27.4.c
First English edition, third printing: London: Thriller Book Club, [1977].

The Blue Hammer

Ross Macdonald

A Lew Archer Novel

**THE THRILLER BOOK CLUB
LONDON**

A 27.4.c: $4^{15}/_{16}'' \times 7^{11}/_{16}''$

A 27.5
Fifth edition: New York, Toronto, London: Bantam, [1977].

#10391-1. Wrappers. Four printings.

A 27.6
Sixth edition: [London]: Fontana/Collins, [1978].

#4588. Wrappers.

Note: *The Blue Hammer* was a Literary Guild alternate selection. Not seen.

A 28 LEW ARCHER PRIVATE INVESTIGATOR

A 28.1
Only edition, only printing (1977)

The Mysterious Press is pleased to announce the publication of:

ROSS MACDONALD'S

LEW ARCHER

Private Investigator

ROSS MACDONALD'S Lew Archer short stories are collected for the first time in this distinguished edition. It is the first complete collection of his Lew Archer stories, and the first hard cover edition. The essay which follows was written expressly as an introduction to the collection. A few copies only of this booklet have been printed for private distribution, prior to the publication of *Lew Archer, Private Investigator*. It is presented with our compliments, to introduce you to this important book.

1977
THE MYSTERIOUS PRESS
New York

NOT FOR SALE

A 28.1: $5^{13}/_{16}'' \times 9''$

[vii–viii] ix–xiii [xiv]

[1]⁴

Contents:　p. vii: title; p. viii: copyright; pp. ix–xiii: introduction by Ross Macdonald; p. xiv: Mysterious Press announcement. First publication of the introduction. See A 29.

Typography and paper:　6³/₁₆″ (6¹/₂″) × 4″. 41 lines per page. Same setting of type as A 29. Wove paper.

Binding:　Beige wrappers with front deckle fore-edge printed in black: Front: [within decorative frame] *ROSS MACDONALD'S* | LEW | ARCHER | Private Investigator'. Back has Mysterious Press device.

Dust jacket:　Published without dust jacket.

Publication:　200 copies. Distributed September 1977. Not for sale. Preceded A 29.

Printing:　Composed by Aspen Press, Boulder, Col.; printed by Universal Lithographers, Baltimore, Md.

Location:　MJB.

ROSS MACDONALD'S

LEW ARCHER

Private Investigator

Front wrapper for A 28.1

A 29 LEW ARCHER PRIVATE INVESTIGATOR

A 29.1.a
First edition, first printing, trade issue (1977)

ROSS MACDONALD'S

LEW
ARCHER

Private Investigator

THE MYSTERIOUS PRESS
New York
1977

A 29.1.a: 5^1/$_2$″ × 8^7/$_{16}$″

Copyright © 1946, 1948, 1953, 1954, 1977 by Kenneth Millar.
Copyright © 1960, 1965 by Ross Macdonald.
Copyright © 1977 by The Mysterious Press.

Grateful acknowledgment is made to the following publications for permission to reprint the stories listed:

Ellery Queen's Mystery Magazine for "Find the Woman" (June 1946) and "Wild Goose Chase" (July 1954)
American Magazine for "The Bearded Lady" (October 1948)
Manhunt for "Gone Girl" (published February 1953 as "The Imaginary Blonde"), "The Sinister Habit" (published May 1953 as "The Guilty Ones"), "The Suicide" (published October 1953 as "The Beat-Up Sister") and "Guilt-Edged Blonde" (January 1954)
Ed McBain's Mystery Magazine for "Midnight Blue" (October 1960)
Argosy for "The Sleeping Dog" (April 1965)

Lew Archer, Private Investigator. Copyright © 1977 by The Mysterious Press. All rights reserved. Printed in the United States of America. No part of this book may be reproduced in any manner whatsoever without written permission except in the case of brief quotations embodied in critical articles and reviews. For information address The Mysterious Press, P. O. Box 334, East Station, Yonkers, N.Y. 10704.

FIRST EDITION

Library of Congress Catalogue Card Number 77-81870
    ISBN 0-89296-033-7 Trade edition
    ISBN 0-89296-034-5 Limited edition

[i–viii] ix–xiii [xiv–xvi] 1–21 [22] 23–51 [52] 53–99 [100] 101–147 [148] 149–245 [246–256]

[A–G]¹⁶ [H]⁸ [I]¹⁶

Contents: p. i: half title; p. ii: blank; p. iii: title; p. iv: copyright; p. v: 'TO JOHN AND ANN AND ADELINE | *Dear in Memory*'; p. vi: blank; p. vii: contents; p. viii: blank; pp. ix–xiii: introduction by Ross Macdonald; p. xiv: blank; p. xv: half title; p. xvi: blank; pp. 1–245: text; p. 246: blank; p. 247: colophon; p. 248: blank; p. 249: 'OTHER BOOKS AVAILABLE FROM | THE MYSTERIOUS PRESS'; p. 250: blank; p. 251: ad for *The King of Terrors;* p. 252: ad for *The Adventures of Herlock Sholmes;* p. 253; ad for *Norgil the Magician;* p. 254: ad for *Kek Huuygens, Smuggler;* pp. 255–256: blank.

    9 stories: "Find the Woman" (C 55), "Gone Girl" (C 61), "The Bearded Lady" (C 57) "The Suicide" (C 64), "Guilt-Edged Blonde" (C 66), "The Sinister Habit" (C 63), "Wild Goose Chase" (C 67), "Midnight Bue" (C 119), "Sleeping Dog" (C 139). See also A 11, A 28.

Typography and Paper: 6³/₁₆″ (6¹/₂″) × 4″. 41 lines per page. Running heads: rectos, story titles; versos, "LEW ARCHER, PRIVATE INVESTIGATOR'. Wove paper.

Binding: Dark gray yellowish brown (#81) V-cloth (smooth). Front: pasted-on white card (3¹/₂″ × 2″) printed in black: 'LEW ARCHER | *Private Investigator*'. Spine gold-stamped: [vertically] *ROSS | MACDONALD* | [line of type decorations] LEW ARCHER |

Private Investigator [line of type decorations] [horizontal Mysterious Press device]. Medium brown endpapers. All edges trimmed. Red and white headbands and footbands.

Dust jacket: Clear plastic; front and back printed in yellow. Front has drawing in yellow of smoking gun.

Publication: 1,000 copies of the trade issue. Published 1 October 1977. $10. ISBN: 0-89296-033-7. Trade and limited issues published simultaneously.

Printing: Composed by the Aspen Press, Boulder, Col.; printed by Universal Lithographers, Baltimore, Md.

Locations: LC (MAR 29 1978; OCT 20 1977 CIP); MJB (dj).

A 29.1.a*
First edition, first printing, limited issue (1977)

[i–viii] ix–xiii [xiv–xvi] 1–21 [22] 23–51 [52] 53–99 [100] 101–147 [148] 149–245 [246–258]

[A–G]^{16} [H]^8 [I]^{16} (I 11+1)

Contents: Same as trade issue, but with certificate of limitation leaf inserted after pp. 245 | 246: 'Of this first edition, | two hundred fifty copies | have been numbered and | signed by the author. | This is copy no.

Typography and paper: Same as trade issue.

Binding: Same as trade issue, but with slipcase in same cloth as binding.

Dust jacket: Same as trade issue.

Publication: Simultaneously published with trade issue. See certificate of limitation. Also 6 numbered but signed copies. $30. ISBN: 0-89296-034-5.

Printing: Same as trade issue.

Locations: Lilly (dj and slipcase); MJB (dj and slipcase); UC-I (dj and slipcase).

A 29.1.b
First edition, second printing: New York: Mysterious Press, 1977.

Not seen.

A 29.1.c
First edition, third printing: New York: Mysterious Press, 1977.

Not seen.

A 29.1.d
First edition, fourth printing: New York: Mysterious Press, 1977.

Not seen.

A 29.2
Second edition: Aftershock | Lew Archer Private Investigator | Police Chief. Roslyn, N.Y.: Detective Book Club, [1978].

Paper-covered boards.

ROSS MACDONALD'S
LEW ARCHER
Private Investigator

by ROSS MACDONALD

The First Complete Collection of Lew Archer Stories

Lew Archer, the quintessential American detective, is the most famous private eye in contemporary mystery fiction.

In the tradition of Raymond Chandler's Philip Marlowe and Dashiell Hammett's Sam Spade, Archer is hard-boiled and philosophical...

ROSS MACDONALD

ROSS MACDONALD is a name in the mystery genre...

CURRENTLY AVAILABLE FROM THE MYSTERIOUS PRESS

The Adventures of Herlock Sholmes by Peter Todd. Introduction by Philip José Farmer. With 19 full-page illustrations by Lewis R. Higgins.
Trade edition (ISBN 0-89296-025-6) clothbound, pictorial dust wrapper, limited to 1,000 copies. $10.00
Limited edition (ISBN 0-89296-026-3) numbered and signed by Farmer, in a custom slipcase, limited to 250 copies. $30.00

Kek Huuygens, Smuggler by Robert L. Fish. Introduction by the author. The complete short adventures of the great rogue, by the creator of *Bullitt*.
Trade edition (ISBN 0-89296-027-2) clothbound, pictorial dust wrapper, limited to 1,000 copies. $10.00
Limited edition (ISBN 0-89296-028-0) numbered and signed by Fish, in a custom slipcase, limited to 250 copies. $30.00

The King of Terrors by Robert Bloch. Introduction by the author. Tales of madness and death by the author of *Psycho*.
Trade edition (ISBN 0-89296-029-9) clothbound, pictorial dust wrapper, second printing. $10.00
Limited edition (ISBN 0-89296-030-2) numbered and signed by Bloch, in a custom slipcase, limited to 250 copies. $30.00

Norgil the Magician by Maxwell Grant. Introduction by the author. Pulp adventures of the magician-detective, by the creator of The Shadow.
Trade edition (ISBN 0-89296-031-0) clothbound, pictorial dust wrapper, limited to 1,000 copies. $10.00
Limited edition (ISBN 0-89296-032-9) numbered and signed by Grant (Walter B. Gibson), in a custom slipcase, limited to 250 copies. $30.00

THE MYSTERIOUS PRESS
P.O. Box 334 East Station
Yonkers, NY 10704

LIMITED EDITION (ISBN 0-89296-034-5)

The Mysterious Press

THE MYSTERIOUS PRESS is a publishing house devoted to mystery, crime, suspense and espionage fiction...

All books published by The Mysterious Press are produced under the editorial direction of Otto Penzler.

THE MYSTERIOUS PRESS
P.O. Box 334
East Station, Yonkers, N.Y. 10704

Dust jacket for A 29.1.a

A 30 A COLLECTION OF REVIEWS

A 30.1.a
First edition, first printing, limited binding issue (1979)

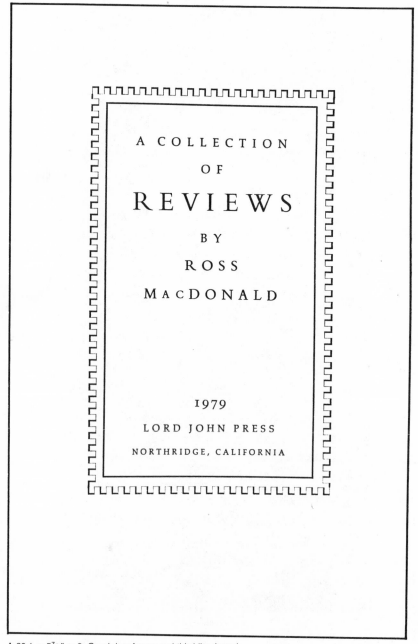

A 30.1.a: 5⁷/₈″ × 9. Greek-key frame and third line in red.

[i–vi] vii [viii] ix–xiii [xiv–xvi] 1–67 [68–72]

[1–3]⁸ [4]⁴ [5–6]⁸

Contents: p. i–ii: blank; p. iii: half title; p. iv: blank; p. v: title; p. vi: copyright; p. vii: contents; p. viii: blank; p. ix–xiii: foreword by Ross Macdonald; p. xiv: blank; p. xv: half title; p. xvi: blank; pp. 1–67: text; p. 68: blank; p. 69: certificate of limitation; p. 70–72: blank.

14 reviews: "The Detective in Fiction" (C 89), "A Catalog of Crime" (C 166), "The Durable Art of James M. Cain" (C 154), "Van Wyck Brooks's Life of W. D. Howells" (C 106), "Strindberg's Love Letters, and Some Other Expressionists," "A New Look at the Tradition of the Novel" (C 93), "England and the Continent," "Studies of the Cultural Revolution in This and Previous Generations" (C 113), "Correspondence of Conrad and His Publishers" (C 92), "T. S. Eliot" (C 104), "The Stature of Colin Wilson (C 110), "Waugh and Peace" (C 188), "Stephen Leacock, Stranger in Paradox" (C 112), "Thomas Mann's Last Words" (C 91). First book publication for all reviews. See appendix 1, note 5.

Typography and paper: 5⁹/₁₆″ (5¹⁵/₁₆″) × 3¹/₂″. Running heads: rectos and versos, title of review. Wove paper.

Binding: Three-piece binding: Medium gray (#265) paper-covered boards with strong red (#12) V-cloth (smooth) shelfback. Front printed in red: '[Greek key frame within 2 single-rule frames] ROSS | MACDONALD | [decoration]'. Spine goldstamped: '[vertically] ROSS MACDONALD • A COLLECTION OF REVIEWS'. Light brownish pink endpapers. All edges trimmed. Red and yellow headband and footband.

Dust jacket: Published without dust jacket.

Publication: 300 numbered and signed copies of the trade issue. Published 25 October 1979. $40. See certification of limitation.

Note: Limited and deluxe binding issues published stimultaneously.

Printing: Certificate of limitation: 'THIS FIRST EDITION of "A COLLECTION OF RE-VIEWS" *is limited to three hundred numbered copies and fifty specially bound deluxe copies, all of which have been signed by the author. The type is Linotype Aldus designed by Hermann Zapf and named for the 16th-century printer Aldus Manutius. The paper is natural Sonata vellum.* | *Designed and printed by Grant Dahlstrom for the Lord John Press.'* | This is number
Location: MJB.

A 30.1.a*

First edition, first printing, deluxe binding issue (1979)

Same pagination and collation as limited binding issue.

Contents: Same as limited binding issue.

Typography and paper: Same as limited binding issue.

Binding: Three-piece binding: red, blue, and yellow marbled paper-covered boards with light blue (#181) V-cloth (smooth) shelfback. Spine goldstamped same as limited binding issue.

Publication: 50 numbered and signed copies. $75. See certificate of limitation.

Printing: Same as limited binding issue.

Locations: MJB; UC-I.

A 31 SELF-PORTRAIT

A 31.1.a
First edition, first printing, limited issue (1981)

SELF-PORTRAIT:
Ceaselessly Into The Past

ROSS MACDONALD

Foreword by Eudora Welty

Edited and with an Afterword by Ralph B. Sipper

CAPRA PRESS
1981
Santa Barbara

A 31.1.a: 6″ × 9″

Cover illustration by Kathleen Mackintosh.
Back cover photograph, courtesy of Ross Macdonald.

Library of Congress Cataloging in Publication Data

Macdonald, Ross, 1915-
  Self-portrait, ceaselessly into the past.

  1. Millar, Kenneth, 1915- —Biography—
Addresses, essays, lectures. 2. Novelists,
American—20th century—Biography—Addresses,
essays, lectures. I. Sipper, Ralph B.
II. Title
PS3525.I486Z47   813'.52 (B)   81-10258
ISBN 0-88496-170-2   AACR2
ISBN 0-88496-169-9 (pbk.)

CAPRA PRESS
Post Office Box 2068
Santa Barbara, CA 93120

[A–F] i–iv [1–2] 3–9 [10] 11–21 [22] 23–37 [38] 39–59 [60] 61–67 [68] 69–79 [80]
81–85 [86] 87–93 [94] 95–107 [108] 109–129 [130–138]

Perfect binding. Unsigned.

Contents: p. A: half title; p. B: epigraph from *The Great Gatsby;* p. C: title; p. D:
copyright; p. E: contents; p. F: blank: pp. i–iv: foreword by Eudora Welty; p. 1: half title;
p. 2: blank; pp. 3–126: text; pp. 127–129: afterword by Ralph B. Sipper; p. 130:
acknowledgments; p. 131: books by Ross Macdonald; p. 132: colophon; pp. 133–136:
blank; p. 137: certificate of limitation: *'Two hundred and fifty copies of this first | edition
have been numbered and signed by | both the author and Miss Welty for Capra Press; |
twenty-six copies in slipcases were also | lettered and signed by both; publication
during | September nineteen hundred and eighty-one. | This is copy';* p. 138: blank.

Includes 21 pieces by Ross Macdonald: "Down These Streets a Mean Man Must Go"
(C 195), "A Collection of Reviews" (foreword to A 30), "Archer in Jeopardy" (foreword
to AA 3), "Lew Archer, Private Investigator" (introduction to A 29), "Kenneth Millar |
Ross Macdonald—A Checklist" (introduction to B 16), "Archer at Large" (foreword to
AA 2), headnote for "Find the Woman" (B 4), "Archer in Hollywood" (foreword to AA 1),
"In the First Person,"† "Writing The Galton Case" (A 25, B 10), "From *South Dakota
Review"* (C 191), "A Death Road for the Condor" (C 134), "Life with the Blob" (C 155),
"Black Tide" (B 17), "An Interview with Ross Macdonald," by Ralph B. Sipper (B 18),
"Great Stories of Suspense" (introduction to A 26), "The Death of the Detective,"†
"Homage to Dashiell Hammett" (C 133), "The Writer as Detective Hero" (A 25, C 138),
"F. Scott Fitzgerald."† Daggers indicate previously unpublished items.

Typography and paper: 7¹/₈″ (7⁷/₁₆″) × 4¹/₄″. 40 lines per page. No running heads.
Wove paper.

Binding: Black Lextone with Morocco-like pattern. Spine goldstamped vertically:
'ROSS MACDONALD~SELF-PORTRAIT [horizontal goat head] CAPRA PRESS'. Red
endpapers. Red and yellow headbands and footbands. All edges trimmed. 26 lettered

copies were issued in a marbled slipcase and with photo of Macdonald and Welty inserted in a pocket on the front pastedown endpaper.

Dust jacket: None.

Publication: Published 30 September 1981. $75 for numbered copies; $150 for lettered copies. Also an unknown number out-of-series presentation copies. ISBN: 0-88496-170-2.

Printing: Composed by Sun Litho National, Van Nuys, Cal.; printed by Bookcrafters, Inc., Chelsea, Mich.

Locations: Lilly (numbered); MJB (numbered, lettered, and out-of-series copies).

A 31.1.a*
First edition, first printing, trade issue (1981)

Same pagination and collation as limited issue.

Contents: Same as limited issue, except that p. 137 is blank.

Typography: Same as limited issue.

Binding: Deep red (# 13) V-cloth (smooth). Spine stamped in black same as limited issue. Black endpapers. Red and yellow headbands and footbands.

Dust jacket: Front lettered in white and black against red; sketch of Macdonald within white oval. Back: inscribed photo of Macdonald.

Publication: 2,841 copies of the trade issue. Published simultaneously with limited issue. $15. ISBN: 0-88496-170-2.

Printing: Same as limited issue.

Locations: MJB (dj), UC-I(dj).

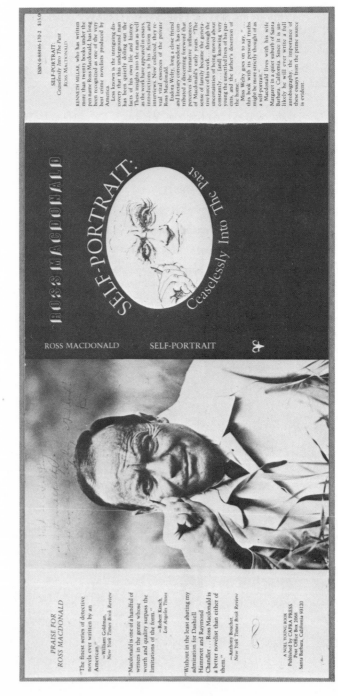

ISBN 0-88496-170-2 $15.00

SELF-PORTRAIT:
Ceaselessly Into The Past
ROSS MACDONALD

KENNETH MILLAR, who has written more than twenty books under the pen name Ross Macdonald, has long been recognized as one of the very best crime novelists produced by America.

Less known is the intriguing discovery that this underground man has been quietly doling out the facts of his own life and history. These insights into the man as well as the work have appeared in essays, introductions to his fiction and interviews. Now collected, they reveal vital essences of the private Ross Macdonald.

Eudora Welty, long a close friend and literary correspondent has contributed a discerning foreword that perceives the formative influences of Macdonald's early years. "The sense of family beneath the generative force of this work... through the uncertainties of being moved about constantly... [and] knowing very young the unsettled lives of his parents, and the father's desertion of the home."

Miss Welty goes on to say... "this book with its personal truths might be more strictly thought of as a self-portrait."

Macdonald lives with his wife Margaret in a quiet suburb of Santa Barbara, California. Since it is unlikely he will ever write a full autobiography, the importance of these essays from the prime source is evident.

ROSS MACDONALD

SELF-PORTRAIT:
Ceaselessly Into The Past

ROSS MACDONALD SELF-PORTRAIT

---

*PRAISE FOR
ROSS MACDONALD*

"The finest series of detective novels ever written by an American."
—William Goldman,
New York Times Book Review

"Macdonald is one of a handful of writers in the genre whose worth and quality surpass the limitations of the form."
—Robert Kirsch,
Los Angeles Times

"Without in the least abating my admiration for Dashiell Hammett and Raymond Chandler... Ross Macdonald is a better novelist than either of them."
—Anthony Boucher,
New York Times Book Review

A NOEL YOUNG BOOK
Published by CAPRA PRESS
Post Office Box 2068
Santa Barbara, California 93120

Dust jacket for A 31.1.a*

A 32 EARLY MILLAR

A 32.1
First edition, only printing (1982)

Early Millar
The First Stories of
Ross Macdonald ❦❦
& Margaret Millar

INTRODUCTORY NOTE
BY ❦ RALPH B. SIPPER

Cordelia Editions
Santa Barbara, California - 1982

A 32.1: 6^1/$_4$″ × 9^5/$_{16}$″. First line and fleurons in red.

[A]¹²

[i–x] 1–10 [11–14]

Contents: pp. i–iv: blank; p. v: title; p. vi: copyright; p. vii: "Introductory Note" by Ralph B. Sipper; p. viii: blank; p. ix: section title; p. x: blank; pp. 1–5: "The South Sea Soup Co." by Kenneth Millar; p. 6: blank; p. 7: section title; p. 8: blank; pp. 9–10: "Impromptu" by Margaret Millar; p. 11: certificate of limitation: 'This first printing of | EARLY MILLAR | consists of 150 numbered copies | designated by Arabic numerals. | There are 15 hardbound Roman numeraled copies | signed by both authors. | Additionally, there are 5 signed hardbound copies | for presentation. | The paper is Mohawk Superfine. | Designed & printed by Patrick Reagh. | This is number   '; pp. 12–14: blank. See C 1.

Typography and paper: 6³/₈″ (7³/₈)″ × 4¹/₈″. 33 or 34 lines per page. Running head: rectos and versos: 'Early Millar'. Wove paper.

Binding: Medium blue (#182) portfolio wrappers. Printed label on front: '[within black single-rule frame] [red] Early Millar | [black] The First Stories of | Ross Macdonald [2 red fleurons] | [black] & Margaret Millar'. All edges trimmed. Also hardbound in full leather.

Publication: Published May 1982. $27.50 for wrappered copies; $225 for leatherbound copies.

Printing: Designed and printed by Patrick Reagh, Los Angeles, Cal.

Locations: MJB (wrappers); Sipper (leather); UC-I (wrappers).

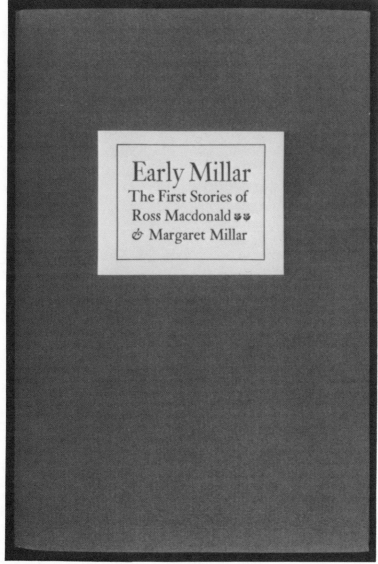

Early Millar
The First Stories of
Ross Macdonald
& Margaret Millar

Front wrapper for A 32.1

AA. Supplement

Collections of Macdonald's Work

AA 1

ARCHER | IN HOLLYWOOD | by *Ross Macdonald* | *With a Foreword by the Author* |
NEW YORK: *Alfred • A • Knopf* 1967 [borzoi device]

On copyright page: 'First Edition'.

Foreword, pp. vii–ix. See A31.

3 novels: *The Moving Target, The Way Some People Die,* and *The Barbarous Coast.*

Reprinted by The Mystery Guild [1967].

AA 2

ARCHER | AT LARGE | *by Ross Macdonald* | *With a Foreword by the Author* | NEW
YORK: *Alfred • A • Knopf* 1970 [borzoi device]

On copyright page: 'First Edition'.

Foreword, pp. vii–xi. See A31.

3 novels: *The Galton Case, The Chill,* and *Black Money.*

Reprinted by The Mystery Guild [1970].

AA 3

ARCHER | *IN* | *JEOPARDY* | *by* | *Ross Macdonald* | THE DOOMSTERS | THE ZEBRA-
STRIPED HEARSE | THE INSTANT ENEMY | With a Foreword by the Author | [borzoi
device] | *Alfred A. Knopf* | *New York* | 1979

On copyright page: 'First Edition'.

Foreword, pp. v-vii. See A31.

Reprinted by The Mystery Guild [1979].

AA 4

Six Great Ross Macdonald Novels [Boxed set of paperbacks]:

The Moving Target. New York, Toronto, London: Bantam, [   ]. #N6793.
The Way Some People Die. New York, Toronto, London: Bantam, [   ]. #N6747.
The Ivory Grin. New York, Toronto, London: Bantam, [   ]. # N6774.

The Chill. New York, Toronto, London: Bantam, [   ]. #N6792.
The Goodbye Look. New York, Toronto, London: Bantam, [   ]. #N5357.
The Zebra-Striped Hearse. New York, Toronto, London: Bantam, [   ]. #N6791.

B. First-Appearance Contributions to Books

B 1 THE QUEEN'S AWARDS
1946

THE | QUEEN'S AWARDS, | 1946 | [decorative wavy rule] | The Winners of the | First Annual Detective Short-Story Contest | Sponsored by | *Ellery Queen's Mystery Magazine* | [decorated wavy rule] | EDITED BY | ELLERY QUEEN | [LB device] | LITTLE, BROWN AND COMPANY • BOSTON | 1946.

On copyright page: 'FIRST EDITION'.

"Find the Woman," pp. 269–292. See C 55.

London: Gollancz, 1947. Not seen.

B 2 MURDER BY EXPERTS
1947

[within frame of wavy rules] Mystery Writers of America | Present | [following 3 line slanted] *MURDER* | *by* | *EXPERTS* | Edited by | ELLERY QUEEN | [Ziff-Davis circular device in bottom line of frame] | [below frame] CHICAGO • NEW YORK

1947.

Headnote by Margaret Millar and Kenneth Millar for William Faulkner's "The Hound," pp. 99–100.

B 3 DISSERTATION ABSTRACTS
1952

Vol. XII   No. 2 | DISSERTATION | ABSTRACTS | (formerly MICROFILM ABSTRACTS) | *A GUIDE TO DISSERTATIONS AND | MONOGRAPHS AVAILABLE IN MICROFORM* | UNIVERSITY MICROFILMS | ANN ARBOR, MICHIGAN: 1952

Abstract of "The Inward Eye: A Revaluation of Coleridge's Psychological Criticism" by Kenneth Millar, p. 190.

Microfilm publication #3533.

B 4 MAIDEN MURDERS
1952

MAIDEN | MURDERS | [rule] | [following 2 lines in script] Mystery Writers | of America | [Harper device] | *Introduction by* | JOHN DICKSON CARR | [rule] | HARPER & BROTHERS NEW YORK

1952.

Kenneth Millar's headnote for "Find the Woman," pp. 97–98.

London: Harmond, Hammond, [1953].

B 5 ELLERY QUEEN'S AWARDS
1954

ELLERY QUEEN'S | AWARDS: | *NINTH SERIES* | [decorated wavy rule] | The Winners of the | Ninth Annual Short-Story Contest | Sponsored by | *Ellery Queen's Mystery Magazine* | [decorated wavy rule] | EDITED BY | ELLERY QUEEN | [LB devce] | LITTLE, BROWN AND COMPANY | BOSTON • TORONTO

1954.

On copyright page: 'FIRST EDITION'.

"Wild Goose Chase" by John Ross Macdonald, pp. 73–98. See C 67.

B 6 A CHOICE OF MURDERS
1958

A CHOICE | *of MURDERS* | *23 stories* BY MEMBERS OF THE | MYSTERY WRITERS | OF AMERICA | EDITED BY | Dorothy Salisbury Davis | NEW YORK | *CHARLES SCRIBNER'S SONS*

1958.

On copyright page: 'A–9.58 [H]'; *'First Edition'*.

Author's postscript for "Guilt-Edged Blonde," p. 63.

B 7 BEST DETECTIVE STORIES OF THE YEAR
1962

Best Detective Stories | OF THE YEAR | *17th Annual Collection* | EDITED BY | BRETT HALLIDAY | [Dutton device] | E. P. DUTTON & CO., INC. | New York   1962

On copyright page: 'FIRST EDITION'.

"Midnight Blue" by Ross Macdonald, pp. 76–114. See C 119.

B 8 BEST DETECTIVE STORIES OF THE YEAR
1966

Best Detective Stories | OF THE YEAR | *21st Annual Collection* | EDITED BY | ANTHONY BOUCHER | E. P. DUTTON & CO., INC. | New York 1966

On copyright page: 'FIRST EDITION'.

"Sleeping Dog" by Ross Macdonald, pp. 235–255. See C 139.

B 9 ESSAYS CLASSIC & CONTEMPORARY
1969

[typographical decoration] ESSAYS | *Classic & Contemporary* | EDITED BY R. W. LID | *San Fernando Valley State College* | J. B. LIPPINCOTT COMPANY | *Philadelphia & New York*

1967.

"The Writer as Detective Hero" by Ross Macdonald, pp. 307–315.

See C 138.

B 10 AFTERWORDS
1968

[two-page title; left] *Novelists on Their Novels* | Edited by Thomas McCormack | HARPER & ROW, PUBLISHERS | New York, Evanston, and London | [right] Afterwords | [circular decoration]

1968.

On copyright page: 'FIRST EDITION'; 'M-S'.

"A Preface to *The Galton Case*" by Ross Macdonald, pp. 146–159.

See A 25, A 31.

B 11 SANTA BARBARA DECLARATION
(1969)

The | SANTA BARBARA | DECLARATION *of* | ENVIRONMENTAL | RIGHTS [cover title of pamphlet includes 5 drawings of flower, fish, birds, and elk in green]

Santa Barbara: January 28 Committee, 1969.

Unsigned, but written by Roderick Nash.

Anonymously edited and co-published by Kenneth Millar.

B 12 DASHIELL HAMMETT
(1969)

[following 3 lines within a 3-sided single-rule frame] Dashiell | Hammett | A CASEBOOK | *William F. Nolan* | with an introduction | by | PHILIP DURHAM | [left of vertical rule] A | LIONS HEAD | BOOK | [right of vertical rule] McNALLY & LOFTIN, *Publishers* | *Santa Barbara*

1969.

On copyright page: 'First printing'.

Anonymously edited by Kenneth Millar.

B 13 MODERN FIRST EDITIONS
1969

MODERN FIRST EDITIONS | AND OTHER BOOKS | LITERARY MATERIAL | FROM MODERN AUTHORS | [8 lines of authors] | SOLD FOR THE BENEFIT OF THE | CENTER FOR EDITIONS OF | AMERICAN AUTHORS | [CEAA seal] | *Public Auction* | *Tuesday Evening* • *December 16 at 8* | PARKE-BERNET GALLERIES • INC | [decorated bracket] *Affiliated with* SOTHEBY & CO: London [decorated bracket] | *New York* • 1969.

Sale #2960.

Facsimile of manuscript page from "Oedipus in Hollywood" (review of *Cain x 3*—see C 154), p. 33, lot 104.

B 14 SANTA BARBARA CITIZENS COMMISSION
1970

SEVENTY-FIVE CENTS | REPORT | OF THE | SANTA BARBARA | CITIZENS | COMMIS- SIONS | ON | CIVIL DISORDERS | *What Occurred?* | *Causes?* | *What Can and Ought to be Done?* | September 15, 1970 Santa Barbara, California.

Cover title.

Kenneth Millar was member of the commission: "I didn't write it, but I filtered nearly all of it."

B 15 CRIMES AND MISFORTUNES
1970

[two-page title; left] [Random House device] RANDOM HOUSE [slash] NEW YORK | [right] [rule] | CRIMES | [rule] | AND | [rule] | MISFORTUNES | [rule] | [following 3 lines in script] The Anthony Boucher | Memorial Anthology | *of Mysteries* | [rule] | Edited by J. Francis McComas

1970.

On copyright page: 'First Printing".

Note on Boucher, p. 210.

B 16 KENNETH MILLAR/ROSS MACDONALD CHECKLIST
1971

ACDONALD KENNETH MILLAR [slash] ROSS MACDONALD KENNETH MILLAR [slash] ROSS MACDONALD | [left: photo of Millar]; [right:] A CHECKLIST | Compiled by Matthew J. Bruccoli | Introduction | by | Kenneth Millar | [logo] A BRUCCOLI [diamond] CLARK BOOK | PUBLISHED BY GALE RESEARCH COMPANY, BOOK TOWER, DE- TROIT, 1971

On copyright page: 'First printing'.

Introduction, pp. xi–xvii; facsimiles of typescripts and manuscripts, pp. 12, 22, 34, 48, 57–58, 61. See A 31, C 175

Note: Some copies of this volume included a 9″ × 3″ white paper bookmark with a 6-line poem by Kenneth Millar headed "To an Unknown Reader" and a facsimile signature in blue.

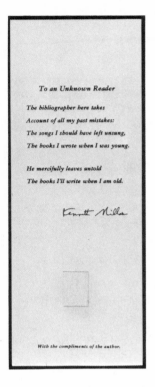

B 17 BLACK TIDE
1972

[2-page title; left] [circular dp device at end of thick and thin rules] | DELACORTE PRESS [slash] NEW YORK | [right] BLACK | TIDE; | [thick and thin rules] | THE SANTA BARBARA OIL SPILL | AND ITS CONSEQUENCES | Robert Easton | *With an Introduction by Ross Macdonald*

1972.

On copyright page: 'First printing'.

Introduction, pp. xi–xvi. See A 31.

B 18 MYSTERY & DETECTION ANNUAL
1973

THE | MYSTERY & DETECTION | ANNUAL | [cat] | DONALD ADAMS | BEVERLY HILLS, CALIFORNIA | 1973

On copyright page: 'First printing'.

Ralph Bruno Sipper, "An Interview with Ross Macdonald," pp. 53–58. See A 31.

Steven R. Carter, "Ross Macdonald: The Complexity of the Modern Quest for Justice," pp. 59–81. Excerpts from letters.

B 19 WORLD AUTHORS
1975

WORLD AUTHORS | 1950–1970 | [tapered rule] | *A Companion Volume to Twentieth Century Authors* | tapered rule] | *Edited by* | *JOHN WAKEMAN* | *Editorial Consultant* | *STANLEY J. KUNITZ* | THE H. W. WILSON COMPANY | New York • 1975

Autobiographical note, pp. 992–993; biographical note on Margaret Millar, p. 994.

B 20 MYSTERY WRITER'S HANDBOOK
1976

MYSTERY | WRITER'S | HANDBOOK | By the Mystery Writers of America | newly revised edition | Writer's Digest | 9933 Alliance Road • Cincinnati, Ohio 45242

1976.

Quotes Macdonald, pp. 11, 23, 31, 58, 186, 264.

B 21 DIMENSIONS OF DETECTIVE FICTION
1976

[within unclosed single-rule frame] LARRY N LANDRUM | PAT BROWNE | RAY B. BROWNE | DIMENSIONS OF | DETECTIVE FICTION | [below frame] [device] | POPU-LAR PRESS

Bowling Green, Ohio: Popular Press, 1976.

Sam L. Grogg, Jr., "Interview with Ross Macdonald," pp. 182–192. See C 179.

B 22 DREAMERS WHO LIVE THEIR DREAMS
1976

Dreamers Who Live Their Dreams: | The World of Ross Macdonald's Novels | *Peter Wolfe* | [device] | Bowling Green University Popular Press | Bowling Green, Ohio 43403

1976. Clothbound and wrappers.

Quotes from letters, pp. 146, 187.

B 23 THREE SANTA BARBARA AUTHORS
1982

[red, blue, gold] THREE SANTA | BARBARA [bird] | AUTHORS & A | BOOKSELLER | RALPH B. SIPPER | CORDELIA EDITIONS | SANTA BARBARA | 1982

"Ross Macdonald: Clues to the Past," pp. 9–14. See C 206.

C. First Appearances in Magazines and Newspapers

C 1

"The South Sea Soup Co., " *The Grumbler* [Kitchener-Waterloo Collegiate and Vocational School] (1931), 23–25.

This burlesque of Sherlock Holmes is KM's first publication. Signed *Ken Miller* [sic]. Also includes Margaret Millar's first published story: "Impromptu" by M. Sturm.

C 2

"Philo France, in the Zuider Zee," *The Grumbler* (1932), 28–30.

Parody. Kenneth Millar and Graham Campbell.

C 3

"To the Damned Their Due . . . ," *The Grumbler* (1932), 63–64.

Story. Kenneth Miller [sic].

C 4

"Kraft's Wooing," *Literary Supplement* [annual supplement to the *University of Western Ontario Gazette*] (20 December 1934), 1, 5.

Story. Ken. Millar.

C 5

"Four Metopes," *Literary Supplement* (18 December 1936), 4.

Prose sketches. Ken Millar

C 6

"Dog Eats Dog," *Literary Supplement* (December 1937), 2.

Unsigned editorial. Millar was an editor for this issue.

C 7

"Renascence in the Morning," *Literary Supplement* (December 1937), 3. Story.

Ken Millar.

C 8

'A Song," *Literary Supplement* (December 1937), 5.

Ken Millar.

C 9

"Free Verse," *Literary Supplement* (December 1937), 5.

Kerith Mill.

C 10
"Three Poems," *Literary Supplement* (December 1937), 5.

George Beale.

C 11
Untitled tribute to John Lee, *The Lyceum [University of Western Ontario Gazette]* (1939), cover.

K. M.

C 12
"A Ballade of Iron Towns," *The Lyceum* (1939), 5.

Poem. Beames Anguish.

C 13
"Fatal Facility," [Toronto] *Saturday Night* 54 (29 July 1939), 20.

Poem. Kenneth Millar.

C 14
"Little Miss Muffet: As T. S. Eliot would have written it; As Walter de la Mare would have written it; As D. H. Lawrence would have written it; As Gertrude Stein would have written it; As W. H. Auden would have written it," [Toronto] *Saturday Night* 54 (12 August 1939), 20.

Poems. Kenneth Millar.

C 15
"A Young Man of Resource," [Toronto] *Saturday Night* 54 (23 September 1939), 24.

Prose sketch. Kenneth Millar.

C 16
"Little Theatre," [Toronto] *Saturday Night* 54 (21 October 1939), 28.

Story. Kenneth Millar.

C 17
"From an Advertising Man's Diary," [Toronto] *Saturday Night* 55 (4 November 1939), 24.

Sketch. Kenneth Millar.

C 18
"The Yellow Dusters," [Toronto] *Saturday Night* 55 (11 November 1939), 24.

Story. Kenneth Millar.

C 19
"Anatomy," [Toronto] *Saturday Night* 55 (25 November 1939), 7.

Poem. Kenneth Millar.

C 20
"Javanese Fairy Tale," [Toronto] *Saturday Night* 55 (23 December 1939), 15.

Review of *Illusion in Java* by Gene Fowler. Kenneth Millar.

C 21
"Short Stories," [Toronto] *Saturday Night* 55 (30 December 1939), 15.

Review of *Love Has No Resurrection* by E. M. Delafield. Kenneth Millar.

C 22
"Time Unheeded," [Toronto] *Saturday Night* 55 (13 January 1940), 20.

Story. Kenneth Millar.

C 23
"Snakes and Ladders," [Toronto] *Saturday Night* 55 (20 January 1940), 9.

Review of *Yesterday's Dreams* by Ruth Feiner. Kenneth Millar.

C 24
"New Life for the Novel," [Toronto] *Saturday Night* 55 (20 January 1940), 28.

Article. Kenneth Millar.

C 25
"Three Epitaphs: Epitaph for a Chef; Epitaph for an Important Man; Epitaph for a Quiet Man," [Toronto] *Saturday Night* 55 (20 January 1940), 28.

Verse. K. M.

C 26
"The Winter Days Pass," [Toronto] *Saturday Night* 55 (10 February 1940), 24.

Poem. Kenneth Millar.

C 27
"Between Wars," [Toronto] *Saturday Night* 55 (17 February 1940), 8.

Review of *Urchin Moor* by Naomi Royde Smith. Kenneth Millar.

C 28
"The Dance," [Toronto] *Saturday Night* 55 (24 February 1940), 32.

Story. Kenneth Millar.

C 29
"Tales and Novellas," [Toronto] *Saturday Night* 55 (2 March 1940), 8.

Review of *Tales Before Midnight* by Stephen Vincent Benet, and *Experiment* by Helen Hull. Kenneth Millar.

C 30
"Caldwell's South," [Toronto] *Saturday Night* 55 (9 March 1940), 9.

Review of *Trouble in July* by Erskine Caldwell. Kenneth Millar.

C 31
"For a Movie Star," [Toronto] *Saturday Night* 55 (16 March 1940), 24.

Poem. Kenneth Millar.

C 32
"For Days the Snow Was Falling," [Toronto] *Saturday Night* 55 (23 March 1940), 3.

Poem. Kenneth Millar.

C 33
"Biography," [Toronto] *Saturday Night* 55 (23 March 1940), 24.

Poem. Kenneth Millar.

C 34
"Trajan," [Toronto] *Saturday Night* 55 (13 April 1940), 28.

Prose sketch. Kenneth Millar.

C 35
"One Man Show," [Toronto] *Saturday Night* 55 (20 April 1940), 13.

Review of *Self Portrait* by Gilbert Frankau. Kenneth Millar.

C 36
"Tragic Prague," [Toronto] *Saturday Night* 55 (27 April 1940), 9.

Review of *A Stricken Field* by Martha Gelhorn. Kenneth Millar.

C 37
"Mr. Hoyberry's Career," [Toronto] *Saturday Night* 55 (27 April 1940), 28.

Prose sketch. Kenneth Millar.

C 38
"Pegasus and the Rocking Horse," *The School* (Secondary Edition) 28 (April 1940), 672–677.

Article. Kenneth Millar.

C 39
"If Light Were Dark,"[Toronto] *Saturday Night* 55 (4 May 1940), 2.

Poem. Kenneth Millar.

C 40
"The Bamboo Crab," [Toronto] *Saturday Night* 55 (4 May 1940), 24.

Prose sketch. Kenneth Millar.

C 41
"Aaland Woman," [Toronto] *Saturday Night* 55 (8 June 1940), 8.

Review of *Mariana* by Sally Salminen. Kenneth Millar.

C 42
"The Man I Meet," [Toronto] *Saturday Night* 55 (22 June 1940), 24.

Prose sketch. Kenneth Millar.

C 43
"Hill Praise," [Toronto] *Saturday Night* 55 (6 July 1940), 20.

Poem. Kenneth Millar.

C 44
"A Hard-Boiled Soft-Boiled Egg," [Toronto] *Saturday Night* 55 (20 July 1940), 24.

Prose sketch. Kenneth Millar.

C 45
"An Enriching Novel of the Irish," [Toronto] *Saturday Night* 56 (28 September 1940), 17.

Review of *Come Back to Erin* by Sean O'Faolain. Kenneth Millar.

C 46
"Contemporary 'Good Talk,' " [Toronto] *Saturday Night* 56 (16 November 1940), 24.

Review of *Rain Before Seven* by John August. Kenneth Millar.

C 47
"For a Modern Cavalier," [Toronto] *Saturday Night* 56 (16 November 1940), 28.

Poem. Kenneth Millar.

C 48
"Alpine Autobiography," [Toronto] *Saturday Night* 56 (7 December 1940), 26.

Review of *Helvellyn to Himalaya* by F. Spencer Chapman. Kenneth Millar.

C 49
"Young Man Goes West," [Toronto] *Saturday Night* 56 (7 December 1940), 27.

Review of *No Steeper Wall* by Percy Marks. Kenneth Millar.

C 50
"Stefansson's Iceland," [Toronto] *Saturday Night* 56 (14 December 1940), 19.

Review of *Iceland* by Vilhjalmur Stefansson. Kenneth Millar.

C 51
"Channel Adventure," [Toronto] *Saturday Night* 56 (28 December 1940), 15.

Review of *Landfall* by Nevil Shute. Kenneth Millar.

C 52
"The Distinguished Canary," [Toronto] *Saturday Night*. Kenneth Millar. Unlocated.

C 53
The following unsigned "The Passing Show" columns in volume 56 of the Toronto *Saturday Night* are "mostly, but not entirely" by Kenneth Millar: 14 December 1940; 4 January 1941; 11 January 1941; 18 January 1941; 25 January 1941; 1 February 1941; 8 February 1941; 15 February 1941; 22 February 1941; 1 March 1941; 8 March 1941; 15 March 1941; 22 March 1941; 29 March 1941; 12 April 1941; all appear on page 3.

C 54
"Thought and English," *The School* (Secondary Edition) 29 (February 1941), 543–545.

Article. Kenneth Millar.

C 55
"Find the Woman," *Ellery Queen's Mystery Magazine* 7 (June 1946), 102–119.

Story. Kenneth Millar. See A 11, A 29, B 1, B 4.

Headnote quotes Millar.

C 56
"The Sky Hook," *American Mercury* 66 (January 1948), 74–79.

Story. Kenneth Millar.

C 57
"The Bearded Lady," *American Magazine* 146 (October 1948), 152–166.

Kenneth Millar. Reprinted as "Murder is a Public Matter," *Ellery Queen's Mystery Magazine* 34 (October 1959).

Story. See A 11, A 29.

C 58
"Blue City," *Esquire* 34 (August–September 1950), 86–96, 94–117.

Condensation of novel. Kenneth Millar. See A 3.

C 59
Verne Linderman, "Good Mysteries Demand Characterization Based on Sound Psychology, Say Millars of Cliff Drive," *Santa Barbara News-Press* (30 March 1952), A-10.

Interview.

C 60
"Shock Treatment," *Manhunt* 1 (January 1953), 71–80.

Story. Kenneth Millar.

C 61
"The Imaginary Blonde," *Manhunt* 1 (February 1953), 1–27.

Story. Kenneth Millar. Reprinted as "The Singing Pigeon," *Manhunt* 12 (May 1964). Collected as "Gone Girl." See A 11, A 29.

C 62
"Experience with Evil," *Cosmopolitan* 134 (March 1953), 129–154.

Condensation of *Meet Me at the Morgue*. John Ross Macdonald. See A 9.

C 63
"The Guilty Ones," *Manhunt* 1 (May 1953), 1–21.

Story. Collected as "The Sinister Habit." John Ross Macdonald. See A 11, A 29.

C 64
"The Beat-Up Sister," *Manhunt* 1 (October 1953), 110–140.

Story. Collected as "The Suicide." John Ross Macdonald. See A 11, A 29.

C 65
Earle F. Walbridge, "Kenneth Millar—'John Ross Macdonald,' " *Wilson Library Bulletin* 28 (December 1953), 334.

Quotes Macdonald.

C 66
"Guilt-Edged Blonde," *Manhunt* 2 (January 1954), 1–12.

Story. John Ross Macdonald. See A 11, A 29, B 6.

C 67
"Wild Goose Chase," *Ellery Queen's Mystery Magazine* 24 (July 1954), 123–141.

Story. John Ross Macdonald. See A 11, A 29, B 5.

C 68
"Find a Victim," *Manhunt* 2 (July 1954), 90–141.

John Ross Macdonald. Reissued in *Giant Manhunt,* no. 4. Condensation of novel. See A 10.

C 68A
Litti Paulding, " 'Lonesomest Job' Loved by Players' Guests," *Santa Barbara News-Press* (23 September 1955), A-6.

Quotes Millar.

C 69
"The Dying Animal," *Cosmopolitan* 140 (March 1956), 84–111.

John Ross Macdonald. Condensation of *The Barbarous Coast.* See A 12.

C 70
"A Critic's Study of the Literary Masters," *San Francisco Chronicle—This World* (30 March 1958), 30.

Review of *Gnomon* by Hugh Kenner. Kenneth Millar.

C 71
"The New Books—Read's Love Affair With Art," *San Francisco Chronicle—This World* (18 May 1958), 26.

Review of *The Tenth Muse* by Herbert Read. Kenneth Millar.

C 72
"A Vein of North Country Iron Runs Through Davie's Poems," *San Francisco Chronicle—This World* (1 June 1958), 25.

Article. Kenneth Millar.

C 73
"Current Fiction Diagnosed—And Other New Literary Pieces," *San Francisco Chronicle—This World* (22 June 1958), 26.

Review of *Man in Modern Fiction* by Edmund Fuller. Kenneth Millar.

C 74

"Passengers on a Cable Car Named Despair," *San Francisco Chronicle—This World* (29 June 1958), 23.

Review of *The Beat Generation and the Angry Young Men,* ed. Max Gartenberg and Gene Feldman. Kenneth Millar.

C 75

"Geismar Has Lost Some of His Fine Enthusiasm," *San Francisco Chronicle—This World* (6 July 1958), 19.

Review of *American Moderns* by Maxwell Geismar. Kenneth Millar.

C 76

"Bridging the Gulf of Descartes," *San Francisco Chronicle—This World* (27 July 1958), 21.

Review of *Existence: A New Dimension in Psychiatry and Psychology* by Rollo May, Ernest Angel, and Henri F. Ellenberger. Kenneth Millar.

C 77

"Guerard—Critic and Novelist," *San Francisco Chronicle—This World* (3 August 1958), 21.

Review of *Conrad the Novelist* by Albert J. Guerard. Kenneth Millar.

C 78

"A Scotsman Surveys British Literary Production," *San Francisco Chronicle—This World* (17 August 1958), 28.

Review of *The Present Age in British Literature* by David Daiches. Kenneth Millar.

C 79

"Notes on Conference of Northwest Writers," *Seattle Times* (17 August 1958), 17.

Interview.

C 80

"The Great Age of Humor," *San Francisco Chronicle—This World* (24 August 1958), 30.

Review of *The Comic Tradition in America,* ed. Kenneth S. Lynn. Kenneth Millar.

C 81

"Among the New Books—Joyce Cary on Life and Art," *San Francisco Chronicle—This World* (7 September 1958), 25.

Review of *Art and Reality* by Joyce Cary. Kenneth Millar.

C 82

"Literary Tributes to Proust—and Other New Books," *San Francisco Chronicle—This World* (14 September 1958), 31.

Review of *Marcel Proust and His Literary Friends* by Laurent Le Sage; *Proust's Way* by Georges Piroue; and *Drieu La Rochelle and the Fiction of Testimony* by Frederic J. Grover. Kenneth Millar.

C 83
"Four New Rising Authors—And a Hunter in Africa," *San Francisco Chronicle—This World* (19 October 1958), 30.

Review of *Short Story I* by Richard Yates, Gina Berriault, B. L. Barrett, and Seymour Epstein. Kenneth Millar.

C 84
Review of *Description of a Struggle* by Franz Kafka. *San Francisco Chronicle—This World* (2 November 1958), 22.

K. M.

C 85
"Women Were Her Sisters in Bondage," *San Francisco Chronicle—This World* (2 November 1958), 28.

Review of *Granite and Rainbow* by Virginia Woolf. Kenneth Millar.

C 86
"Morris—The Territory Ahead Is Always Behind Us," *San Francisco Chronicle—This World* (28 December 1958), 15.

Review of *The Territory Ahead* by Wright Morris. Kenneth Millar.

C 87
"Literary Studies of Proust and Maugham," *San Francisco Chronicle—This World* (18 January 1959), 15.

Review of *Marcel Proust* by Richard H. Barker; *Proust Recaptured* by Pamela Hansford Johnson. Kenneth Millar.

C 88
"Lifting the Mask of England"s Comic Literary Genius,' *San Francisco Chronicle—This World* (15 February 1959), 26.

Review of *Evelyn Waugh* by Frederick J. Stopp. Kenneth Millar.. See A 30.

C 89
"Research Into the History of Detective Fiction," *San Francisco Chronicle—This World* (15 Feburary 1959), 29.

Review of *The Development of the Detective Novel* by A. E. Murch. Ross MacDonald. See A 30.

C 90
"The Biographer Could Not Forgive Poe His Foolishness," *San Francisco Chronicle—This World* (8 March 1959), 23.

Review of *The Haunted Palace* by Frances Winwar. Kenneth Millar.

C 91
"The 'Last Essays' of Thomas Mann," *San Francisco Chronicle—This World* (2 April 1959), 35.

Review of *Last Essays* by Thomas Mann. Kenneth Millar. See A 30.

C 92
"The New Books—A Fascinating Three-Way Correspondence," *San Francisco Chronicle—This World* (19 April 1959), 24.

Review of *Joseph Conrad: Letters to William Blackwood and David S. Meldrum,* ed. William Blackburn. Kenneth Millar. See A 30.

C 93
"A Young Critic Rediscovers the Great Russian Tradition," *San Francisco Chronicle—This World* (19 April 1959), 25.

Review of *Tolstoy or Dostoevsky* by George Steiner. K. M. See A 30.

C 94
"A Rolfe Romance—and Other New Books," *San Francisco Chronicle—This World* (3 May 1959), 28.

Review of *Nicholas Crabbe* by Frederick Rolfe. Kenneth Millar.

C 95
"A Friend and Associate Recalls Joyce Cary," *San Francisco Chronicle—This World* (5 May 1959), 37.

Review of *Joyce Cary* by Andrew Wright. Kenneth Millar.

C 96
"Collected Criticism of Conrad Aiken," *San Francisco Chronicle—This World* (24 May 1959), 23.

Review of *A Reviewer's ABC* by Conrad Aiken. Kenneth Millar.

C 97
"Mauriac's Surgery on the Contemporaries . . . ," *San Francisco Chronicle—This World* (31 May 1959), 17.

Review of *The New Literature* by Claude Mauriac. Kenneth Millar.

C 98
"The Prose Poet Who Remained a Boy at Heart," *San Francisco Chronicle—This World* (14 June 1959), 24.

Review of *Kenneth Graham* by Peter Greene. Kenneth Millar.

C 99
"The New Books—Contributions to the Theory of Tragedy," *San Francisco Chronicle—This World* (19 July 1959), 22.

Review of *The Vision of Tragedy* by Richard B. Sewall; *The Question of Hamlet* by Harry Levin. Kenneth Millar.

C 100
"A Shelf of Philosophical Books—Kierkegaard to Weber," *San Francisco Chronicle—This World* (2 August 1959), 18.

Review of *Irrational Man* by William Barrett; *Man and Crisis* by José Ortega y Gasset; *Consciousness and Society* by H. Stuart Hughes. Kenneth Millar.

C 101
"Studies on French Writing and a Life of Oscar Wilde," *San Francisco Chronicle—This World* (6 September 1959), 20.

Review of *Proust* by George D. Painter; *The Art of French Fiction* by Martin Turnell; *So Be It, Or the Chips Are Down* by André Gide; *Oscar Wilde* by Frank Harris; *A Concise Survey of French Literature* by Germaine Mason. Kenneth Millar.

C 102
"The Populist Platform—Study of Influence and Contradiction," *San Francisco Chronicle—This World* (20 September 1959), 24.

Review of *America's Literary Revolt* by Michael Yatron. Kenneth Millar.

C 103
"Dr. Dorous Sets Lectures Here on Medical Hypnotism," *Santa Barbara News-Press* (30 September 1959), C-4.

Article. Kenneth Millar.

C 104
"A California Critic Raises Eliot Into Clearer Visibility," *San Francisco Chronicle—This World* (4 October 1959), 25.

Review of *The Invisible Poet* by Hugh Kenner. Kenneth Millar. See A 30.

C 105
"Among the New Books—A Brilliant American Anthology," *San Francisco Chronicle—This World* (25 October 1959), 28.

Review of *The Chicago Review Anthology,* ed. David Ray. Kenneth Millar.

C 106
"Howells Represented America to Itself and the World," *San Francisco Chronicle—This World* (8 November 1959), 24.

Review of *Howells, His Life and World* by Van Wyck Brooks. Kenneth Millar. See A 30.

C 107
"New Books . . . ," *San Francisco Chronicle—This World* (15 November 1959), 34.

Review of *Joseph Conrad* by Osborn Andreas.

K. M.

C 108
"A Collection of Thoreauvian Correspondence and Studies," *San Francisco Chronicle—This World* (15 November 1959), 36.

Review of *The Correspondence of Henry David Thoreau,* ed. Walter Harding and Carl Bode, and *A Thoreau Handbook* by Walter Harding. Kenneth Millar.

C 109
William Hogan, " 'The Unspeakable Calamity'—To Be Without Books," *San Francisco Chronicle—Christmas Books* (22 November 1959), 3.

Includes Kenneth Millar's list of recent books he particularly enjoyed.

C 110
"Colin Wilson Romps Again in Rocky Philosophical Pastures," *San Francisco Chronicle—This World* (29 November 1959), 19.

Review of *Stature of Man* by Colin Wilson. Kenneth Millar. See A 30.

C 111
"A Frenchman's Reflections on Literature and Morality," *San Francisco Chronicle—This World* (13 December 1959), 42.

Review of *Pretexts: Reflections on Literature and Morality* by Andre Gide. Kenneth Millar.

C 112
"Leacock Loved and Ornamented the Anglo-Canadian Language," *San Francisco Chronicle—This World* (3 January 1960), 21.

Review of *Stephen Leacock: Humorist and Humanist* by Ralph L. Curry. Kenneth Millar. See A 30.

C 113
"Changing Culture—Innocence's End," *San Francisco Chronicle—This World* (10 January 1960), 24.

Review of *Culture in Private and Public Life* by F. R. Cowell; *The End of American Innocence* by Henry F. May; *The West-Going Heart: A Life of Vachel Lindsay* by Eleanor Ruggles. Kenneth Millar. See A 30.

C 114
"Bibliography of a Major California Novelist—and Other Books," *San Francisco Chronicle—This World* (7 February 1960), 28.

Review of *Frank Norris: A Bibliography* by Kenneth A. Lohf and Eugene P. Sheehy. Kenneth Millar.

C 115
"Menninger Adds to Understanding," *Santa Barbara News-Press* (17 April 1960), B-8.

Review of *A Psychiatrist's World* by Karl Menninger. Kenneth Millar.

C 116
"The Brontes—Through Anne's Unblinking Eyes," *San Francisco Chronicle—This World* (15 May 1960), 27.

Review of *Anne Bronte* by Ada Harrison and Derek Stanford. Kenneth Millar.

C 117
"A Seaman, Genius and Scoundrel Shed Light on a Literary Era," *San Francisco Chronicle—This World* (29 May 1960), 21.

Review of *Joseph Conrad* by Jocelyn Baines; *Stephen Crane: Letters,* ed. R. W. Stallman and Lillian Gilkes; *Frank Harris* by Vincent Brome. Kenneth Millar.

C 118
"A Search for the Constraining Forces in American Fiction," *San Francisco Chronicle—This World* (24 July 1960), 22.

Review of *Love and Death in the American Novel* by Leslie Fiedler. Kenneth Millar.

C 119

"Midnight Blue," *Ed McBain's Mystery Magazine* 1 (October 1960), 2–24. Ross Macdonald.

See A 29, B 7.

C 120

Maurice Dolbier, "About the Millars of Santa Barbara," *New York Herald Tribune Book Review* (13 November 1960), 2.

Based on interview.

C 121

Martha MacGregor, "The Art of Writing About Murder," *New York Post Week-end Magazine* (27 November 1960), 11.

Interview.

C 122

Letter to the editor, *Santa Barbara News-Press* (8 February 1961), D-8.

Kenneth Millar.

C 123

"Take My Daughter Home," *Cosmopolitan* 150 (April 1961), 102–126.

Condensation of *The Wycherly Woman*. Ross Macdonald. See A 16.

C 124

"Crime and Chaos," *New York Post* (20 August 1961), sec. 11.

Review of *Kidnap* by George Waller. Ross Macdonald.

C 125

"Bring the Killer to Justice," *Ellery Queen's Mystery Magazine* 39 (February 1962), 18–32, 62–80, 107–117.

Condensation of *The Doomsters*. Ross Macdonald. See A 13.

C 126

"A Zebra-Striped Hearse," *Cosmopolitan* 203 (September 1962), 102, 104–106, 108–129.

Condensation of novel. Ross Macdonald. See A 17.

C 127

Letter to the editor, *Santa Barbara News-Press* (19 November 1962), B-18.

Kenneth Millar.

C 128

Letter to the editor, *Santa Barbara News-Press* (24 January 1963), B-16.

Kenneth Millar.

C 129

Robert F. Jones, "A New Raymond Chandler?" *Los Angeles Magazine* 5 (March 1963), 58–59.

Interview.

C 130
"The Chill," *Cosmopolitan* 155 (August 1963), 106, 108–129.

Condensation of novel. Ross Macdonald. See A 18.

C 131
Letter to the editor, *Santa Barbara News-Press* (18 September 1963), E-8.

Kenneth Millar.

C 132
Letter to the editor, *Santa Barbara News-Press* (31 December 1963), B-12.

Kenneth Millar.

C 133
"Homage to Dashiell Hammett," *Mystery Writers' Annual* (1964), 8, 24.

Article. See A 31. Ross Macdonald.

C 134
"A Death Road for the Condor," *Sports Illustrated* 20 (6 April 1964), 86–89.

Article. Ross Macdonald. See A 31.

C 135
"The Far Side," *Cosmopolitan* 157 (September 1964), 100, 102–109, 111–117, 121–130.

Condensation of *The Far Side of the Dollar*. Ross Macdonald. See A 19.

C 136
Heather Burn, "Interview with an Author," *John O'London's Books of the Month* (November 1964), 10.

C 137
Letter to the editor, *Santa Barbara News-Press* (17 December 1964), D-12.

Kenneth Millar.

C 138
"The Writer as Detective Hero," *Show* 5 (January 1965), 34–36.

Articles. Ross Macdonald. See A 25, A 31, B 9.

Also note by Macdonald, p. 4.

C 139
"The Sleeping Dog," *Argosy* 360 (April 1965), 42–43, 90–95.

Story. Ross MacDonald [sic]. See A 29, B 8.

C 140
"Murder in the Library," *Mystery Writers' Annual* (1965), 2.

MWA presidential statement. Kenneth Millar.

C 141
Martha MacGregor, "The Week in Books," *New York Post* (9 May 1965), 49.

Interview.

C 142
"Prizes and Awards," *Publishers Weekly* 187 (10 May 1965), 43.

Includes Macdonald statement.

C 143
"The Demon Lover," *Cosmopolitan* 159 (December 1965), 110–118, 120–133, 136–139.

Condensation of *Black Money*. Ross Macdonald. See A 20.

C 144
Jack Jones, "Writer Keeps One Eye on Novel, Other on Sparrow," *Los Angeles Times* (4 January 1966), sec. 3, 1, 4.

Quotes Millar.

C 145
Letter to the editor, *Santa Barbara News-Press* (16 February 1966), D-10.

Kenneth Millar.

C 146
The Crime Writer 14 (5 May 1966).

Autobiographical note.

C 147
Letter to the editor, *Santa Barbara News-Press* (24 October 1966), C-12.

Kenneth Millar.

C 148
Letter to the editor, *Santa Barbara News-Press* (7 September 1967), C-8.

Kenneth Millar.

C 149
Dick Adler, "Will the Real Ross Macdonald Please Keep Writing?" *Los Angeles Times West* (10 December 1967), 79–80, 82–83, 85–86.

Interview.

C 150
"The Slow Death of the California Condor," *San Francisco Chronicle—This World* (12 May 1968), 34.

Review of *Man and the California Condor* by Ian McMillan. Kenneth Millar.

C 151
Letter to the editor, *Santa Barbara News-Press* (27 May 1968), C-10.

Kenneth Millar.

C 152
"Eddie's Story," *New York Times Book Review* (22 September 1978), 8.

Review of *Brief Against Death* by Edgar Smith. Ross Macdonald.

C 153
Letter to the editor, *Santa Barbara News-Press* (30 October 1968), F-10.

Kenneth Millar.

C 154
"Cain × 3," *New York Times Book Review* (2 March 1969), 1, 49–51.

Review of *Cain × 3* by James M. Cain. Ross Macdonald. See A 30.

C 155
"Life with the Blob," *Sports Illustrated* 30 (21 April 1969), 50–52, 57–60.

Article. Ross Macdonald. See A 31.

C 156
Letter to the editor, *Santa Barbara News-Press* (11 May 1969), A-15.

Kenneth Millar.

C 157
John Leonard, "Ross Macdonald, his Lew Archer and other secret selves," *New York Times Book Review* (1 June 1969), 2, 19.

"Profile of Ross Macdonald," a *Collins News Bulletin* (1969 press release), is based on this interview.

C 158
Letter to the editor, *Life* 67 (4 July 1969), 16-A.

Kenneth Millar.

C 159
"Santa Barbarans Cite an 11th Commandment: 'Thou Shalt Not Abuse the Earth,' " by Ross Macdonald and Robert Easton, *New York Times Magazine* (12 October 1969), 32–33, 142–149, 151, 156.

Article. Ross Macdonald.

C 160
Letter to the editor, *Santa Barbara News-Press* (9 January 1970), C-10.

Kenneth Millar.

C 161
Gian Franco Orsi, "Chi e Ross Macdonald," *Il Giallo Mondadori* 1,114 (7 June 1970), 179–183.

Interview in Italian based on written replies.

C 162
Letter to the editor, *Santa Barbara News-Press* (17 June 1970), H-12.

Kenneth Millar.

C 163
"The Underground Man," *Cosmopolitan* 170 (February 1971), 172–176, 178, 180, 184, 186–190, 192, 194–204.

Condensation of novel. Ross Macdonald. See A 23.

C 164
Raymond Sokolov, "The Art of Murder," *Newsweek* 77 (22 March 1971), 101–102, 104, 106, 108.

Profile of Ross Macdonald based on interviews.

C 165
"Don't Shoot—We Are Your Children!" *New York Times Book Review* (25 April 1971), 5.

Review of *Don't Shoot—We Are Your Children* by J. Anthony Lukas. Ross Macdonald.

C 166
"A Catalogue of Crime," *New York Times Book Review* (16 May 1971), 3.

Review of *A Catalogue of Crime* by Jacques Barzun and Wendell H. Taylor. Ross Macdonald. See A 30.

C 167
Martha MacGregor, "The Week in Books," *New York Post Magazine* (29 May 1971), 15.

Interview.

C 168
B. A. B. [Barbara Bannon], "Authors & Editors," *Publishers Weekly* 200 (9 August 1971), 19–20.

C 169
John Barkham, "Where Writing is No Mystery," *New York Post Magazine* (21 August 1971), 15.

Interview.

C 170
F. R. [Frances Ring], "By Any Other Name," *Westways* 63 (September 1961), 2, 4.

Interview.

C 171
Peter Preston, "The Farther Side of the Dollar," *Manchester Guardian* (23 October 1971), 9.

Interview.

C 172
Philip Oakes, "In For Life," *London Sunday Times* (24 October 1971), 33.

Interview.

C 173
William Foster, "The Private Eye Tradition," [Edinburgh] *Scotsman* (20 November 1971), weekend section, 1.

Interview.

C 173A
Ed Wilcox, "The Secret Success of Kenneth Millar," *New York Sunday News* (21 November 1971), 158–159.

C 174
"An Interview with Ross MacDonald," *Concept Twelve* (1971), 33–45.

C 175
"Millar/Macdonald Defines a Life of Criminal Writings," *Los Angeles Times Calendar* (16 January 1972), 1, 15, 24–25.

Introduction to *Checklist*. Kenneth Millar. See A 31, B 16.

C 176
"Goldenrod,' *New York Times Book Review* (11 June 1972), 6, 29.

Review of *Goldenrod* by Herbert Harker. Ross Macdonald.

C 177
Jon Carroll, "Ross Macdonald in Raw California," *Esquire* 77 (June 1972), 148–149, 188.

Interview.

178
"Beautiful Books About Terrible Things," *Detroit News* (22 October 1972), 5-E.

Review of *Graham Greene, The Entertainer* by Peter Wolfe. Ross Macdonald.

C 178A
Letter, *Saturday Night* 88 (March 1973), 3.

Kenneth Millar.

C 178B
"A Conversation with the Author," *Santa Barbara News & Review* (23 March 1973), 7.

C 179
Sam Grogg, Jr., "Ross Macdonald: At the Edge," *Journal of Popular Culture* 7 (Summer 1973), 213–222.

Interview. See B 21.

C 180
Letter, *New York Times Book Review* (5 August 1973), 24.

Ross Macdonald.

C 181
Robert A. Wright, "Broad Spectrum of Writers Attacks Obscenity Ruling," *New York Times* (21 August 1973), 38.

Includes Macdonald statement.

C 182
Burt Prelutsky, "Big Fish in the Big Pond," *Los Angeles Times Calendar* (25 November 1973), 18.

Interview.

C 183
Beverly Jackson, "The Award Was a Mystery," *Santa Barbara News-Press* (6 February 1974), B-8.

Interview.

C 184
Cecil Smith, " 'Underground Man' to Surface on TV," *Los Angeles Times* (9 March 1974) sec. 4, 12.

Interview.

C 185
Cecil Smith, "Is Archer a Cop? 'Yes, Ma'am, the Private Form,' " *San Francisco Sunday Examiner & Chronicle Date Book* (14 April 1974), 28.

Interview.

C 186
Brad Darrach, "Ross Macdonald: The Man Behind the Mysteries," *People 2 (8 July 1974), 26–30.*

Interview.

C 187
Jerry Tutunjian, "A Conversation with Ross Macdonald," *Tamarack Review* 62 (1974), 66–85.

C 188
Chuck Thegze, "Behind Lew Archer: Interview with Ross Macdonald," *Village Voice* (10 February 1975), 27.

C 189
Marshall Berges, "Margaret Millar & 'Ross Macdonald,' " *Los Angeles Times Home* (29 June 1975), 22–23, 27.

Interview.

C 190
Charles Champlin, "Here Today, Gone Tomorrow," *Los Angeles Times* (4 July 1975), sec. 4, 1, 25.

Interview.

C 191
Contribution to symposium on "The Writer's Sense of Place," *South Dakota Review* 13 (Autumn 1975), 83–84.

Ross Macdonald. See A 31.

C 192
Trevor Meldal-Johnsen, "Ross Macdonald," *Gallery* 4 (March 1976), 84–88, 90.

Interview.

C 193
Celeste Durant, "Ross Macdonald: After 19th Novel," *Chicago Sun-Times Living* (28 July 1976), 69, 74.

Interview.

C 193A
Clifford A. Ridley, "Yes, Most of My Chronicles Are Chronicles of Misfortune," *National Observer* (31 July 1976), 17.

C 194
John Hemsley, "The Private Life of a Private Eye," *Belfast Telegraph* (17 September 1976), 2.

Based on an interview.

C 195
"Down These Streets a Mean Man Must Go," *Anataeus* 25–26 (Spring/Summer 1977), 211–216.

Essay. Ross Macdonald. See A 31.

C 196
Beverly Slopen, "The Most Private Eye," *Toronto Star Canadian* (20 August 1977), 9–10.

Interview.

C 197
Peter Gardner, "Happy Moments at the Mailbox," *Bookviews* 1 (September 1977), 13.

Includes statement.

C 198
"The Private Detective," *New York Times Book Review* (23 October 1977), 2, 40–41.

Introduction to *Lew Archer, Private Investigator*. Ross Macdonald. Preceded by A 28.

C 199
"Writers' Writers," *New York Times Book Review* (4 December 1977), 62.

Includes statement on Nelson Algren.

C 200
Brian Garfield, "The State of the Art," *Publishers Weekly* 213 (13 March 1978), 51.

Contribution to symposium.

C 201
Richard R. Lingeman, "Book Ends," *New York Times Book Review* (2 April 1978), 47.

Interview.

C 202

"Booze & the Writer," *Writer's Digest* 58 (October 1978), 26–27.

Includes statement.

C 203

"The Books That Made Writers," *New York Times Book Review* (25 November 1979), 84.

Reply to: "What book made you decide to become a writer and why?"

C 204

Gene Davidson and John Knoerle, "Ross Macdonald Interview," *Mystery* 1 (November-December 1979), 5–8.

Interview.

C 205

Ann Japenga, "The Millars: A Cooperative Success," *Los Angeles Times* (20 December 1979), sec. 4, 32.

Interview.

C 205A

Mickey Friedman, "The First Family of Mystery Writing," *San Francisco Examiner* (19 May 1980), 24.

C 206

Ralph Sipper, "The Faces of Ross Macdonald," *Santa Barbara* 6 (Winter 1980), 66–69.

Quotes Macdonald. See B 23.

C 207

Jane S. Bakerman, "A Slightly Stylized Conversation with Ross Macdonald," *Writer's Yearbook 1981*, 52 (1981), 86, 88–89, 111.

D. Blurbs

Statements written by Macdonald to promote
works by other authors, arranged alphabetically.

D 1

Thomas Berger, *Sneaky People* (London: Magnum, 1980).

Statement in ad: *Bookseller* (12 January 1980), 154.

D 2

Andrew Bergman, *The Big Kiss-Off of 1944* (New York: Holt, Rinehart & Winston, 1974).

Statement in ad: *New York Times* (28 March 1974), 37.

D 3

Andrew Bergman, *Hollywood and LeVine* (New York: Holt, Rinehart & Winston, 1975).

Statement in ad: *New York Times Book Review* (13 July 1975), 18.

D 4

Anders Bodelson, *Straus* (New York: Harper, 1974).

Statement in ad: *The New Yorker* 50 (13 May 1974), 158.

D 5

Matthew J. Bruccoli and Jennifer Atkinson, *As Ever, Scott Fitz—* (Philadelphia & New York: Lippincott, 1972).

Statement in ad: *New York Times Book Review* (30 July 1972), 14.

D 6

Matthew J. Bruccoli and Margaret M. Duggan, eds., *Correspondence of F. Scott Fitzgerald* (New York: Random House, 1980).

Statement about Bruccoli's *Scott and Ernest* (New York: Random House, 1978) on dust jacket.

D 7

Raymond Chandler. Statement on front covers of the Ballantine editions of *Killer in the Rain, Trouble Is My Business, The Simple Art of Murder, Playback, The Long Goodbye, Pickup on Noon Street.*

From introduction to B 16.

D 8

Francis Clifford, *Good-bye and Amen* (New York & London: Harcourt Brace Jovanovich, 1974).

Statement on dust jacket.

239

D 9

Michael Collins, *Act of Fear* (New York: Dodd, Mead, 1967).

Statement on dust jacket. Also on dust jackets of Collins's *Night of the Toads* (New York: Dodd, Mead, 1970), Collins's *Shadow of a Tiger* (New York: Dodd, Mead, 1972), and William Arden's *A Dark Power* (New York: Dodd, Mead, 1968).

D 10

John Crowe, *Bloodwater* (New York: Dodd, Mead, 1974).

Statement on dust jacket.

D 11

Peter Dickinson, *The Glass-Sided Ants' Nest* (New York: Harper & Row, 1968).

Statement on dust jacket. Also on wrapper: New York: Ace, 1969. #28960.

D 12

Lesley Egan, *The Borrowed Alibi* (New York: Harper, 1962).

Statement on dust jacket.

D 13

Robert Emmitt, *The Legend of Ogden Jenks* (New York: Ballantine, 1971).

Quote from *San Francisco Chronicle* review on wrapper. #02442-7-095.

D 14

Dick Francis, *Nerve* (New York & Evanston: Harper & Row, 1964).

Statement on dust jacket.

D 15

Leonard Gardner, *Fat City* (New York: Farrar, Straus and Giroux, 1969).

Statement on dust jacket. Also statement in ad: *New York Times Book Review* (24 August 1969), 15; also first page: New York: Dell, 1970. #2480.

D 15A

James Goldman, *Waldorf* (New York: Random House, 1965).

Statement in ad: *New York Times Book Review* (7 November 1965), 80.

D 16

William Goldman, *The Princess Bride* (New York: Harcourt Brace Jovanovich, 1973).

Statement in ads: *New York Times* (21 September 1973), 39; 3 December 1973, 36; 31 October 1973, 42.

D 17

Herbert Harker, *Goldenrod* (New York: Random House, 1972).

Quote from *New York Times* review in ads: *New York Times* (19 June 1972), 31; 10 July 1972, 29; also on dust jacket of Harker's *Turn Again Home* (New York: Random House, 1977).

D 18
George V. Higgins, *The Friends of Eddie Coyle* (New York: Knopf, 1972).

Statement in ads: *New York Times* (1 February 1972), 35; 22 February 1972, 35.

D 19
Joan Kahn, ed., *The Edge of the Chair* (New York: Harper & Row, 1967).

Statement on dust jacket. Also statement in ad: *New York Times Book Review* (15 October 1967), 9.

D 20
Joan Kahn, ed., *The Midnight Raymond Chandler* (Boston: Houghton Mifflin, 1971)

Statement in Book-of-the-Month Club mailer. Also statement in ads: *New York Times Book Review* (5 December 1971), 50; *The New Yorker* 47 (18 December 1971), 135.

D 20A
Ed Lacy. *The Men from the Boys* (New York: Harper, 1956).

Statement on dust jacket flap.

D 21
George Lanning, *The Pedestal* (New York: Harper & Row, 1966).

Statement on dust jacket.

D 22
Michael Z. Lewin, *The Enemies Within* (New York: Knopf, 1974).

Statement on dust jacket.

D 23
Michael Z. Lewin, *Night Cover* (New York: Knopf, 1976).

Statement on dust jacket.

D 24
Michael Z. Lewin, *The Silent Salesman* (New York: Knopf, 1978).

Statement on dust jacket. Also statement in ad: *The New Yorker* 58 (27 March 1978), 136.

D 25
Desmond Lowden, *Bellman & True* (New York: Holt, Rinehart & Winston, 1975).

Statement on dust jacket. Also statement in ad: *New York Times* (27 July 1975), 35.

D 26
J. Anthony Lukas, *Don't Shoot—We Are Your Children* (New York: Dell, 1972).

Statement from *New York Times* review on wrapper. #2125.

D 27
Frank MacShane, *The Life of Raymond Chandler* (New York: Dutton, 1976).

Statement in ad: *Publishers Weekly,* 209 (1 March 1976), 3.

D 28

William McIlvanney, *Laidlaw* (New York: Pantheon, 1977).

Statement on dust jacket. Also on wrapper on Popular Library edition (New York, 1979). #0-445-04334-2.

D 29

William F. Nolan, *Dashiell Hammett A Casebook* (Santa Barbara, Cal.: McNally & Loftin, 1969).

Statement on dust jacket. See B 12.

D 30

Roger Simon, *The Big Fix* (San Francisco: Straight Arrow, 1973).

Statement in ad: *New York Times* (11 September 1973), 42. Also on wrapper of Pocket Books edition (New York, 1974). #77746.

D 31

Edgar Smith, *Brief Against Death* (New York: Avon, 1969).

Quote on wrapper from *New York Times* review. #W157.

D 32

Robert Kimmel Smith, *Ransom* (New York: McKay, 1971).

Statement in ad: *New York Times Book Review* (13 June 1971), 28. Also on wrapper of Signet edition (New York, 1972). #Q5047.

D 33

Raymond Sokolov, *Native Intelligence* (New York: Harper & Row, 1975).

Statement on dust jacket.

D 34

Chris Steinbrunner and Otto Penzler, *Encyclopedia of Mystery & Detection* (New York: McGraw-Hill, 1976).

Statement in mailer.

D 35

Julian Symons, *Mortal Consequences* (New York: Harper & Row, 1972).

Statement on dust jacket. Also on wrapper of Schocken edition (New York, 1973).

D 36

Julian Symons, *The Players and the Game* (New York: Harper & Row, 1972).

Statement on dust jacket. Also on wrapper of Avon edition (New York, 1975). #25106.

D 37

Gerald Walker, *Cruising* (New York: Stein & Day, 1970).

Statement on dust jacket.

D 38
Douglas Wallop, *Howard's Bag* (New York: Norton, 1973).

Statement in ad: *New York Times Book Review* (1 April 1973), 18.

D 39
Collin Wilcox, *Long Way Down* (New York: Random House, 1974).

Statement in *Mystery Guild Clues* (August 1975). Also on wrapper of Jove edition (New York, 1979). #M5195.

Appendices / Index

Appendix 1

Compiler's Notes

1. Foreword to *Archer at Large:* "I aimed lower, at tortoise level, writing a flock of short stories and sketches for quickly available Toronto markets, most of which were so-called Sunday School papers paying a cent a word. I made over a hundred dollars the first few weeks." Millar recalls three stories—"Marilyn Misses the Picnic," "Abernathy the Squirrel," and a story about an Irish family in Donegal. None of these publications has been located.

2. Film. *Ross Macdonald—"In the first person"* (John M. Davidson, 1970). Written by Kenneth Millar and Arthur Kaye; directed and produced by Kaye. See A31.

3. Film. *Ross Macdonald* (Educational Broadcasting Corp., 1977). Produced by Richard Moore.

4. Unpublished dissertation. Kenneth Millar, "The Inward Eye: A Revaluation of Coleridge's Psychological Criticism," University of Michigan, 1951. See B3.

5. Previous publication for two of the book reviews in *A Collection of Reviews* (A30) has not been located: "Strindberg's Love Letters, and Some Other Experiments," "England and the Continent."

6. "Good and Helpful Book on Psychiatry," *Santa Barbara News-Press* (unlocated). Review of *Master Your Tensions and Enjoy Living Again* by George S. Stevenson and Harry Milt. Kenneth Millar.

7. Millar has said that the first thing he ever sold was a piece about typing, based on a quotation from Sir Charles G. D. Roberts (Jerry Tutunjian, "A Conversation with Ross Macdonald," *Tamarack Review* 62 [1974], 72). Unlocated.

Appendix 2

Books and Articles About Macdonald

Bruccoli, Matthew J. *Kenneth Millar/Ross Macdonald: A Checklist*. Detroit, Mich.: Bruccoli Clark/Gale Research, 1971.

Sokolov, Raymond A. "The Art of Murder," *Newsweek* 77 (22 March 1971), 101–104, 106, 108.

Speir, Jerry. *Ross Macdonald*. New York: Ungar, 1978.

Wolfe, Peter. *Dreamers Who Live Their Dreams: The World of Ross Macdonald's Novels*. Bowling Green, Ohio: Bowling Green University Popular Press, 1976.

Index

Pittsburgh Series in Bibliography